It Was *Love* that Kept Me Going

IRENE GUTIERREZ

Order this book online at www.trafford.com
or email orders@trafford.com

Most Trafford titles are also available at major online book retailers.

Printed in the United States of America.

ISBN: 978-1-4669-6488-4 (sc)
ISBN: 978-1-4669-6487-7 (e)

Trafford rev. 10/20/2014

www.trafford.com

North America & international
toll-free: 1 888 232 4444 (USA & Canada)
fax: 812 355 4082

A heart felt story about 2 young boys doing whatever it took to help their mother overcome her arthritis pain.

Contents

Acknowledgements

I would first "love" to thank God for bringing me this far, for helping me and guiding me through this process. It's the first time I have ever written and it was fun because I love writing. It also opened a lot of closed wounds. However, I had a lot of love and support throughout this project, which made things easier on me.

Now I want to thank my two very handsome boys, Thomas Elijah and James Lee, for their outstanding work on helping me get through my very tough times. I had a lot of medical help, but the most critical was the help I got in the middle of the night and very early mornings. That came from my two little helpers that God gave me. My two boys, they are what is most precious to me.

I would like to thank my family for taking time to help me, whether it was helping me physically or just with a warm phone conversation. My work family, I work with great people who showed lots of love and concern for me. Thank you for all your help. I would also like to thank my wonderful customers who made my job so easy. All of these people have become part of my life.

To the church reverend, and his wife for being the first to read my book and giving me all the advice I needed. Being a former book publisher, his advice really came in handy. Answering any questions I had over the phone, even if he was on his way out the door. Thank you!

Another HUGE thanks and that would be for Ashley Leal. For her speediness on the keyboard and for knowing me, by only having seen me from a distance, but agreed to type my entire book for me. Way to go Ashley and thanks to her parents Joe and Linda Gusman.

The Purpose of my Book

I wrote this book is for a couple of reasons. One is to let people know that no matter how hard things get for someone, you can come out of it with prayer and determination and not giving up. It's not easy. I hit rock-bottom and didn't think that I would ever get back on my feet. I asked a lot of people for help, and I thought that's the way it was going to be for the rest of my life. When you're down and stressed, negative thoughts will cross your mind. Just keep telling yourself that you are determined to make things better and that things will get better. You have to start taking baby steps again but its okay. I wanted to change my life years ago, so I did something about it. Now I want another change, but this time I made it easier for myself. Especially to all the single mother's and father's out there, you can do it. Set your mind to it and feel good about knowing that you're on your way to making a change and just keep that positive attitude. Keeping a positive attitude will help you get so far. First, you have to love yourself, and then show your children how much you love and care for them. That alone should motivate you and allow you to do anything you want to. Pray and do your part of the work and leave the rest to god.

My name is Irene Gutierrez. This is my story, and I want to share it with you. It is about the past 10 years of my life. I think after reading this book you will feel like you have lived with me, and know what I've been through. It's about becoming a single mother in 2002, raising two little boys in a tough neighborhood and living with Rheumatoid Arthritis.

I'm in pain every day, and it's been years since I can remember a normal day without pain. I knew I was hurting one day, but was unsure of what it was. It was definitely something I had never felt before. I ignored it the first few days but then quickly realized the pain was not going away. I am a retail employee, working with the public and trying to hide my pain was easy to do at first. I just took over the counter pain medicine which seemed to be working for me, but not for long. What did help me was the love that came from my two little boys. Two very young boy's in elementary school. But what they did for me was the most awesome job in the world.

The Beginning of the End

It was the summer of 2002, a hot miserable time in my life. Things were only about to get worse. My kids were 3 and 5 years old, and about to start public school. My 3 year old would be turning 4 in August and making him right on time to go to school. Their dad and I had a very bad relationship, but it hadn't always been that way. Things started spinning out of control and heading downhill fast. I tried to save my relationship with counseling but I guess it just wasn't meant to be. Then right before school started; sure enough I knew things had to come to an end. But oh my gosh, what was to come next came full force. I left and was staying here and there with my kids and it was getting old. My car was barely making it. I had two babies and asking around every day, "Is it okay if we stay here tonight, we just need one night and we will be gone in the morning." I began asking everybody every single day for just one night's stay. It was a horrible feeling.

No Money

I never in my wildest dreams thought I would ask someone I hardly knew to help feed my kids. There's a restaurant between my sister's house and the Day Care they used to go to. My kids knew when we were getting close. We always went the same way. It killed me to know that my kids were going to ask me for breakfast on the way to Day Care and I had no money.

Before we went to bed that night, sure enough my children asked me if we were going to the restaurant in the morning. I said "Yes, now go to sleep."

I couldn't go to sleep thinking about me telling them, "Yes". They are just going to remind me in the morning.

I thought, "Should I ask my sister?" No! I had already spent the night there. (Many nights) What do I do now? I just couldn't go to sleep. Then I thought of something. I remembered that every time I go there, there's always the same girl. Maybe she will be there tomorrow. I really didn't know her that well, but I knew of her because she had helped me before in the mornings. I was hoping she would remember me too because I was always ordering the same thing. I finally went to sleep. Just knowing I was going to ask that young lady in the morning for help really bothered me, but deep inside I knew I had to try anything. I just couldn't believe I was going to ask someone I hardly knew to provide breakfast for my children. I was embarrassed and angry at the same time.

When morning came, it seemed like we were the only ones on the road. I knew she drove a blue mustang. I arrived to the restaurant hoping to see her car, but also dreaded seeing it. I had a lot of mixed feelings. I was just hoping she would give my children something for the trip. When I arrived I saw her car and as I pulled up to the window, there she was. Okay, part of my misery was over.

I started off by saying something like "Oh, I'm so glad it's you, I'm really embarrassed to ask but, is there any way you could help me out by giving me breakfast for my kids? I have no money and just need to get them a little something, I promise to come back and pay you".

She never hesitated, she immediately said, "Oh yes, what do they want?" I think I remember her saying that she would put it on her meal ticket, but I could be wrong. Finally after stressing all night, it was over. *Thank you god.*

As I was getting ready to drive off she said, "If you need anything for your boys, let me know. Or if they need breakfast." *Thank you god.* Something finally went right for me.

I will never forget what she did for me and I never let the boys forget about her. They knew her name, and they knew of her, but really didn't know who she was. About 8 or 9 years passed before I took the boys over to her house to meet her. It was emotional for me. Sometimes you will cross roads you never imagined crossing. But when it comes to your kids, as a mother you will do it. You might feel embarrassed at the moment. In the long run your children will thank you, and then you will feel nothing but joy.

I had my family, but they were too far away from the school so I couldn't ask. I had already stayed with my sister before so I didn't want to ask her again. I avoided asking my parents because I had already stayed there on and off when I was having problems. But I knew I had a house so I kept going back home because I didn't want to be there with two kids. But then things got really bad and eventually I had to leave. Soon I ran out of places to stay and found myself *feeling* homeless. I went to a certain person's house thinking I could stay the night and be gone in the morning. So I get there, talked a little, and I kicked my shoes off and she looked at me in a strange way. She left the room and came back a few minutes later shouting (not in a bad way) my kid's names. "Tommy, James let's go."

She looked at me and my heart dropped. She said "Are you ready Irene?"

"Ready for what?"

"I'm going to give you guys a ride."

I said, "Well, where are you taking us?" I didn't say another word. I just put my shoes on, got my kids and got in her car. She took me to my sister's house, but no one was home at the time. I got my kids and got out of the car anyway. We just waited in her garage. It had open doors on each side.

There is a saying people say, "We got caught in a storm." Well, we did get caught in a storm, a real storm. It happened shortly after we got dropped off. I know now that my sister was running late and would never make it back to her house until after 10:30 that night. As we we're waiting in the garage it started to get colder and darker, the wind started picking up, then it started thundering and lighting and shortly after that the rain started. My boys were so scared. I picked them up; they dug their faces into my neck. I held one with each arm. I said something I should not have said because my kids never forgot it for a long time.

I started crying and I said "I can't believe this, we're f#$%^n homeless." I stood there holding the kids, finally the storm passed after about 25 minutes which seemed like hours. My sister never made it, but a friend of hers happened to come by and she gave me and my kids a ride to my other sister's house. My sister could not believe it. She ordered us a pizza then made up a bed for us.

There were a few good things that happened to us. (Laughing) But like everyone else she had her family and again I had to start looking for us another place to stay. I could have stayed with a couple of friends, but when I looked into it either someone was already staying with them, or the moment was just not right. My sister's house was too far from the school. A couple other places didn't work out either because of the distance. Not too much help from their dad, and that's where a lot of my anger was. But, going forward, weeks went by then months. It was a horrible time for us. I never thought I would sleep in so many places. I think that's why today my kids and I are so close. We were always together sleeping in small spaces or all three of us on a couch. I was in other people's houses so I made sure I kept my babies close to me. Sometimes it would be close to midnight before I could find a place for us to stay. But I just continued to pray and God always made it possible for me to find us a place to sleep.

A Big Relief

One day after months of bouncing from house to house I went to eat dinner at my mom's house. We sat there, it started getting late and she said, "You and the boys come to this room and lay down." Before I could say another word she said, "And tomorrow I will move this stuff from here so you can bring your stuff and put it here. This room can be for you and the boys."

Hallelujah!! We had a place to stay! Now I just had to continue finding rides in the morning to get the boys to school. I started volunteering in Tommy's class so I quickly made a lot of friends with the moms and asked them if they could pick us up in the morning. I said I don't have any money but I could fix them a plate of food. No problem. Now I had a ride. Soon I went to get in line for what was humiliating for me. But I had to for the sake of my kids. FOOD STAMPS. Yes, I applied for welfare. I started getting food stamps and had no choice but to do that.

I could not be there and expect them to dish out meals for us also. I just couldn't believe all this was happening to me. It was very stressful because you can't just sit there, cry, and expect room service. You have to think 24/7 and act quickly.

Once I got settled in I started as soon as possible to look for ways to get me back on my feet. I at least wanted to have an apartment or car lined up for when I did get some money. That didn't always work, but I would quickly think of something else. Please don't let your mind come to a dead end, just keep going. Stop and cry if you have to its okay its part of it. Let it out then get back to it. You will be glad you did. I knew I could find a job; I just didn't have a car. I couldn't get a car because I had no money to buy one. That's where my other big problem was.

Asking for rides all the time just wasn't going to get it. It takes a lot out of you and not only that, it gets old. People soon start dodging you. Thinking you're going to ask them for a ride again. There were some people that were genuinely nice people to me; they would stop by my mom's in the evening to see if I had a ride. I never passed those up. I didn't have a cell phone to keep people's names and numbers, but a pen and a sheet of paper does the job just as well. Think of anything that will make things easy for you and it will also help you be less stressed.

A Good Poor Girl

I'm a good poor girl, it was very hard and very depressing but I never stopped looking and I never stopped praying. My sister that ordered pizza for us would always tell me, "Don't worry Irene GOD has a job for you." I had always worked, so believe it or not I didn't want to hear her. "Thank him for the job he already has for you".

I rolled my eyes. "Yeah, okay." I would think that's real easy for her to say. But it wasn't what I wanted to hear. Then where is it? I told her you have a car, a job, a house and a husband. But she only meant well.

She invited me over to eat later that week so me and my kids went and had dinner. She asked how things were going and I said "The same." There she goes again.

"It's going to be okay Irene, God has a job for you, just thank him".

Finally a few days later I get a car. (A used one of course) I would ask God for anything, so like they say be careful what you wish for you just might get it. It was a 91 Caprice, no hubcaps, wrecked, hail damage but the sucker worked. It turned out to be the best car and I used it for 4 years. I was so happy to have a car I was no longer going to ask for rides.

I got it late at night when my kids were asleep at my mom's. Morning came I said, "Okay boys lets go to school."

There goes Tommy, "Where did you find a ride so early?" I showed them the car, they were so happy. It was our home away from my mom's house. I would come home at night just in time to give the boys a bath and go to bed. By sunrise we were gone.

Blessings can be anything and anywhere. When I moved out I had to get rid of a few things so I gave a lady my grill because she had no stove. She was so excited about the grill and kept thanking me. People have told me that you can walk straight into a blessing without knowing. You just happen to be at the right place at the right time.

A Horrible experience

After being excited every day about having a car, I would let my kids go back over to my sister's house across town. I would pick them up after work. This would take place on the weekends. After picking them up, I got on to a busy road, Granbury Rd. The boys of course were strapped in the back.

It was night time and it was a cold night. But that's not the only thing I clearly remember. As I drove down the road, I heard a pop sound. I thought of course it was a blow-out. My steering wheel never shook and the car was running smooth. Then I recognized the sound, I was hearing the "road", the back door had come wide open. The worst feeling ever. I closed it; I know I closed it right. James was asleep.

Tommy said calmly, "Mom the door opened". I almost broke my arm, swinging it back and telling Tommy to hold on to my hand, but to stay strapped in. In an instant twenty things crossed my mind. I took my foot off the gas pedal. Bad traffic, what do I do? What if the truck behind us hits us for slowing down? I only tapped on the break. I didn't want to slam them in fear that it would jerk and scare Tommy more. It was his side that came open. All this time my emergency lights are on. Hoping to slow traffic behind me. I tried staying calm, but how does a mother stay calm when the back door comes open and her two babies are back there. I finally come to a light.

Everyone was stopped. In an instant Tommy slams the door and locks it. He unstrapped James and dumped him over the front seat. Then, he crossed over to the front. It happened so fast. I had already taken my seat belt off to turn and get the baby but Tommy had already dumped him over. The best feeling ever. Better than winning the lottery. I don't know what it feels like to win the lottery, but nothing can be better that your children beside you safe.

Then, I couldn't stop shaking. The rest of the way home I kept thanking God. I just kept saying, thank you God, thank you God. My sister still lives in the same house and when we go over, I can't help but think of what happened on that road. James doesn't remember a thing, but Tommy does. You know Tommy. Please let this serve you as an eye opener. Never let your babies or children go unstrapped. If they go to sleep in the car, lean their head in and not towards the door in case of an accident. But remember you don't need something horrible to happen to you to thank God. Just do it. I never took this as a bad omen, the car turned out to be the best car. Remember, *If God is with us, who can be against us?*

Getting a Job

Very shortly after I got the car I had said I would do two things. Renew my shopping card and buy Tommy a birthday cake since I was unable to do that on his birthday. So we drive down to the warehouse, did what I was going to do and got Tommy a round Spiderman cake. I had him inside the basket. We were in line to pay and Tommy was so excited he told the lady passing by, "Hey, look at my cake!"

She said, "How cool is that?"

So, we talked for a good few minutes about Tommy's age and if he was going to school. Then she says, "I'm sorry, I don't mean to keep you, and I'm taking your time."

"Oh, you are not taking my time I have all the time in the world."

Then she said, "If you have all the time in the world, why don't you come work for us? We're hiring cashiers."

A big light came on when she said that and I immediately remembered my sister saying, *"Thank God for the job he already has for you"*.

I said "Oh really?" so she gave me her name and number.

"Give me a call if you decide you want to work."

I said "Oh, I can tell you right now I want to work." So she set up an interview with me, couple days later I was working there, making more money than I ever had.

When I got hired on I called my sister she said, "*Ya ves manita* (you see little sis), you just have to have faith."

It was great working and knowing that *I* was providing for my children. I had been so broke for so long. I remember my first check was $85.00, and I was so happy. Who cares what the amount was, I was working and I had a check. Things got better and better financially. So that's what I mean when I say don't give up. Little by little things will work out. Just continue to push yourself.

Another Downfall

Our personnel office was upstairs, I remember going up the stairs and thinking, man it really hurts when I try going up stairs. I didn't know yet that it was arthritis. I just knew that it hurt. It never stopped me from going to work. I know for sure I didn't have it the first year that I worked there. I'm certain I had it the following year. I felt terrible, that I was asking my kids to help me in and out of the car. What I mean by that is, I would get my right leg in and sit down. Then my oldest would help me with my left leg. I couldn't move it. My oldest would then get in and he could do his own seat belt but before I got in I had to strap James in.

Seems like my condition worsened as the weeks passed. I had a very hard time getting in and out of bed. I would just pray and ask God to give me the strength I needed to keep going. I couldn't have anything on the floor that would be in my way of walking. Early in the morning and late at night were the hardest for me. It would hurt if I moved it with my foot. Every path had to be clean for me. Scooting over a shoe or a backpack gave me a stabbing pain.

The results: Rheumatoid Arthritis. I felt like I was on to something since I had a name to go with my pain and somehow it just made me feel a little more at ease knowing what it was. When people asked I would tell them and they would tell me that I was too young for arthritis, I was about 35. My mother has it and I have known of younger who suffer with it as well. My niece was diagnosed at the age of 3. I'm so glad I have it this severe and not them.

The pain was more than I could handle. I clearly remember it was very cold outside and when we were waiting for the results I was crying. I didn't know what it could be. Why did I suffer with severe pain? A very tall doctor comes in and says, "Your results are back, its rheumatoid arthritis."

My mom felt so bad, but I said, "It's okay mom."

She said, "You got that from me."

Oh well, I'm short also like her too. I also have very premature grey hair, she better be glad I love her.

I went to so many emergency rooms after that. They had already told me it was arthritis, but I just kept thinking that there had to be a mistake. It was only because the pain I had was so severe.

There were days I could barely walk. Getting up early in the morning, especially in the winter, was brutal for me. I had mats right next to my bed. I would slide off the bed in tears and just slowly start stretching and moving my legs and arms. I tried to do it silently where the boys wouldn't hear me. Then I would go to the kitchen and scoot a chair over by the refrigerator, get an ice pack, and sit there for about 15 or 20 minutes icing my knee and my shoulder. Then I took a hot shower. I took my time to do all of that. Then I started getting ready for work. That's the reason why I didn't think it was arthritis and I was just hoping that another doctor would tell me something different. After every check-up and blood work, they would just tell me that there's nothing wrong.

I just had some inflammation from the arthritis, which was good news, it should be what people want to hear. But in my case, because of the pain I wanted them to find something. By that I mean, I wanted them to tell me I had a torn ligament or something. Go in and do surgery and be done. No! Not that easy.

So, deep inside, I would start feeling depressed again. I would just think to myself, *"There's that answer again. Nothing. Then why can't I walk? Why is it so difficult and painful to get up in the morning? Why does every step I take hurt me? Why?"*

When I was at my worse, I would pray so hard, asking God not to take me yet. I really thought I was going to die. I never wanted to leave my boys. I almost wanted to be mad at God. One of those crazy thoughts went through my mind. I just kept thinking, God knows I'm a single mother, he knows they need me. I'm the one that works and I stand up all day. Why would he let this happen to me? I do know that there are people out there even worse than me, so I tell myself, *"Don't ask just stay strong, keep praying."* It's the best thing anyone can do.

Neighborhood Mom's

I met some really great moms when my kids were in elementary school. Mothers that kept a very close eye on their kids and most of them were stay at home moms with working husbands. I would tell my kids to go to Ivan's house and wait there until I get off work. Sometimes they didn't want to go to the after school program. Then I would call Ivan's house, talk to his mom and tell her that my boys would be going by there.

Ivan's mom never said no. My kids were welcome there any day at any time. If Ivan did not come home on time, she would call me. I would let her know if he was with my son. The mother's would call and say, "Tyler is on his way to your house, can you please call me when he gets there."

I did the same thing. My Tommy would go to his friend Danny's house; his mom would call me and tell me, "Did you know Tommy is over here?" If one kid didn't show up on time, we would all start making phone calls. It just seems funny to me now, how even my kid's friends had their turn in helping me, either in or out of the car or up the stairs into my house. Oh, my kids would get so mad at me if I asked one of them for help.

Tommy would often say, "Mom, we're here, ask us."

I didn't care who it was, I was going to hold on to the closest one to me. The mothers would also feel so bad for me. Just like the store customers. They would also give me remedies on how to feel better. A lot of home remedies were very similar. Some remedies I just couldn't quite understand like rubbing "lighter fluid" on my skin.

No, that one I just couldn't do. I just had severe arthritis and nothing really seemed to help me. I just kept asking for prayers. There's nothing better than that. Take it from me. Find you a nice spot at home; make it your everyday praying spot. You will find yourself wanting that spot more and more.

There is a guy who lives in front of me; it is a small white house very similar to the one I am living in now. He is a great neighbor. When the boys were younger he would play football with them in the street. I would be sitting in the living room, not watching, but listening to them laughing and running in the street.

My neighbor's parents live on the corner house next to my neighbor but their house faces a different direction. That house has a corner window that I love because you can see strait to my house. They would also let me know what the boys were doing when I wasn't there. The boys didn't like it, but it gave me piece of mind when I was at work. We have our own little neighborhood watch, and it helps. My neighbor always gave my boys good advice about what they should and shouldn't do. I thank God every day for putting great people in my path. It will happen for you as well.

Entertainment

When my kids were in pre-school, I took them for a snow-cone one day in the summer. The snow-cone stand was across the street from a big park. The park had a big swimming pool. Kids were splashing, swimming and jumping off the diving board.

My son said, "Mom, can we go there?"

I kept it in mind. One day, I bought them some swimming trunks and I took them. I remember after going there a couple of times, the boys just kind of splashed around and never really left my side. They were too young so I had to get in also. I would carry James in the water and just walk around the pool with him. I took lunch one day; I just figured we would spend the day out there. Tommy, my oldest took a break from the water to eat. James and I stayed in the water.

As I was holding him I said, "Kick your feet."

He was loving it. I said now move your hands like this. I showed him how to move them and twenty minutes later he was swimming on his own. Not perfect, but he was doing it. I told Tommy, "Look Tommy, he is swimming on his own!" I was so excited and clapping.

Tommy puts his food down, jumps in the pool and says, "Teach me mom."

They both learned how to swim on the same day. I even documented the day. After years of going there, I could finally stay out of the water. I would take a chair and just watch from a distance, from two ft. to eleven ft. and jumping off the diving board. I thought that it was pretty neat.

I got in every now and then because by this time I had arthritis. I didn't at first. After a while my kids were embarrassed because we didn't have a folding chair. It was just a plastic lawn chair.

After swimming we always got something to eat. They hated going through a drive through window because of the big chair we had in the car, oh well that was then. I'm telling you, I made do with what I had and at that time, I had lawn chairs; not folding chairs.

One thing we all loved after swimming was the warm car when we were right out of the pool. The first couple of minutes in a hot car are okay. Any longer we were not going to find out, but we sure loved that. Restaurants are always cold to us. After leaving restaurants again we always look forward to those first 2 minutes in the car. We don't recommend everyone doing that, that's just us.

That big plastic chair came in handy. If the boys wanted to go to the park, I would take it. As my arthritis got worse, it put a lot of limits on things. I use to pitch baseballs to the boys, a little football too, they really enjoyed that. I enjoyed doing that for them too but, it soon had to come to a stop, it really bothered me because it seemed like little by little I was stopping myself from doing a lot of things.

It saddened me, but I still pushed myself to do as much as I could. I would have to explain to them that I wanted to do more with them but that mama was hurting and couldn't do it. Tommy always said its okay. James really didn't have an answer but he was almost 2 years younger so not much mattered to him. I was just glad to be able to drive and take them places and entertain them. They remember and are grateful today.

Pizza and games were at the top of their list. My sister and I took them together with her kids. It was a place for them to run, jump and climb and have a good time. That's exactly what we all did. I also took them to the Go-carts. They loved that fast ride; my kids of course were not tall enough to ride them on their own so I had to ride with them. One at a time. The man working there always watched the other kid for me. All my other son would do was stand against the fence and watch until it was his turn.

Then he wanted two rides which meant four rides for me. Not a good feeling. Let me tell you, it was not the easiest way to entertain them. Those go-carts are like sitting on the ground, so low. I had to do it, I didn't have a choice at first. After they passed that line and were tall enough, just like the swimming pool, they were on their own. I took them and watched. They even rode 3 or 4 times in a row, I didn't care. I wasn't doing it. They were doing it. They were the ones having a good time. My baby boy was tall enough to ride one year before his older brother. Then he helped me by giving Tommy rides. That was so funny.

Raising My Kids over the Phone

I really felt like part of my kids childhood was me talking to them over the phone. I loved early morning shifts because then I could be there for them in the afternoon. When they were in elementary I had them go to an afterschool program. They would watch them for me until I got there. It was a big help, they had their days when they liked going, then there were days where they just begged me to take them somewhere else for a couple of days. I do feel like I was destined to live where I live because it was close to the school, close to the afterschool program and in case of emergency, close to my parent's house. Then my other small problem was that my kids didn't have a cell phone when they were younger, I could not afford to have 3 cell phones at one time.

I would call the afterschool program and I would ask Tommy "Have you see your brother?"

"Yes he is here"

"Tell him to do his homework".

"Okay, I will mom"

"Did you do your homework Tommy?"

"Yes, I mean no, well I'm working on it, but I want to do it at home. Can you come get us? I don't like this food, and I'm hungry. Mama did you have a good day?"

That sweet little question always made me tear up.

Any chance I got I would call the person watching them. "Are they okay? Do you know if both of them are there or just one of them?"

Then the babysitter replied, "No just Tommy."

I would call the house down the street. "Hi, this is James's mom, just wondering if James is there with your son."

"Yes, he is here".

Thank you God. My heart would immediately go back in place. One day the afterschool program called me to work and said Tommy was at school, but never made it on the van. He was in 3rd grade. I started making phone calls.

I called all my numbers shaking and hoping the first person would say, "Yes, he is here!" but nothing, no luck. No one seen him, all the mothers would start making phone calls.

One of them noticed my shaky voice and said "Don't worry, let me go drive around".

Sure enough Tommy was sitting on our porch waiting for me. When I talked to him he said "You were crying this morning mama, so I didn't get on the van, I wanted to see you so that you don't cry" after a short pause he asked, "Am I in trouble?"

What do you say to that? So the babysitter calls and tells me I will go get James and you can pick both of them up from my house when you get off work.

Sometimes my kids would use their friend's cell phone to call me.

"Hi mama, are you almost off?" Tommy would say.

"Almost baby, where are you?"

"I'm at the babysitters"

"No Tommy, you are not supposed to be there today."

"Oh, I know but I learned my way over here. So here she wants to talk to you."

My son James was running towards me one day after school. He then must have been in second or third grade.

"Mama, mama you know how to feel better? My teacher said you have to be skinny. Just be skinny and now you don't have Arthur-itis"

I didn't know what to say. I just looked around for his teacher but I said "Do what baby? Be skinny? I already tried that." It's been a few years and I'm still trying. Still trying and still praying, that people can find an easier way to help themselves live with Rheumatoid arthritis or whichever one they have. There are over 100 types of arthritis. I guess for now just keep donating to the arthritis foundation.

Home Remedies

S o many customers would tell me about home remedies that they knew about. I know that if they gave me two thousand remedies I can say I tried 17 hundred of them, minus the lighter fluid one. I'm being sarcastic on the numbers I just mentioned, at first there were very many remedies given to me.

Sometimes I wouldn't even be thinking about the pain I would just be working. The way people would ask me, it just seemed like they felt so sorry for me.

They would ask, "Where do you hurt?" or "You look like your hurting real bad." or even "Are you going to be okay you look pale."

I will never forget the day they told me I looked pale, I actually felt pretty good that day. Most of my co-workers have really been good to me. I was recently going down stairs and this lady that works with me was at the bottom of the stairs. She kept looking at me as I came down; I was holding a till with my money. She asked me, "Do you need help?"

I said, "No thanks, I'm okay."

Then she said, "Well I'm gonna stay right here and watch you, I'm not leaving until you make it down"

Going down stairs is easier than going up stairs. My friends see me and say, "Why don't you take the elevator."

"Because if I'm in a hurry then I will just take the stairs."

I'm lucky to have so many people care about me. Including my ex mother in law. I never married my kid's father but I knew I would have a great mother in law if I did. To this day she has been a great mother in law to me and a great grandmother to my boys. She also gives me remedies and always keeps me and the boys in her prayers.(mami)

Most every customers that goes to my job knows me and know about me having arthritis. Sometimes they can throw me off. I will be walking and someone will ask, "How is your leg feeling today" and seems to me like I have never even seen that person before in my life.

Obviously I must have told them one day, because how else would they know. It's okay at least their asking. Then there are the days when I think I'm doing good and then someone will ask. "Why are you limping?"

So I asked my chiropractor, he said it's called muscle memory. My body is so used to it that I think I'm doing well but other people will notice the limping is still there.

My boys walk with me in the afternoon and they tell me, "Put your foot all the way down and don't turn your hip so much." Or, "Quit looking down just think about nothing hurting you". We have a good time; I told them I will be well one day. James gets impatient quick and Tommy just takes his time with me, he does have a lot of patience when it comes to us doing our own home therapy. I wish I had more time for therapy. That is what my leg really needs, but I just don't have all the time I need.

I'm sure there are a lot of working mothers out there that feel the same way I do, and some that work even harder. I know I'm not the only working woman with arthritis and I applaud those women who do work with arthritis. I never even thought I would go to a chiropractor. I was 43 I believe at the time and I just love him. He knew I was low on money and he still took care of me. It made the biggest difference on the first day. I recommend chiropractors.

A Mother's Wish

I truly wish my boy's the best of luck as they get older. I want them to be successful in whatever it is they choose to be in life. Tommy did not play enough football in school but, he would have loved to have gone to the NFL. He played in elementary, middle school and a little bit in school. His coaches really liked him and said he had a lot of potential but he ended up not playing the rest of his freshman year. He also loves the barber trade.

James loves the military and loves reading about people who served in the military thirty and forty years ago. My dad served in the U.S army and I love to see his pictures. My boy's think it is so cool that he served.

Arthritis has devastated me, but I have not let it get me down. Not all the way. I support my kids 100% and hope they do well in the future. I always ask God to guide them in the right direction. My next goal is for "me" to serve my kids.

Don't get me wrong I have raised my kids and did what all I could do for them. There was a lot I missed because I was either working or in bed sick. My family that lives close to me, helped me anyway they could. My mom would call me and tell me to stop by after work so that she could rub an ointment that she had, or they would just pick a day to walk with me at the park across the street from my mom's house. My brother in law and his family helped me a lot. Thank you will never be enough.

There were early morning phone calls to my sister, "Hey, can you come and take me to the hospital, I'm in a lot of pain I can't even make it to the car." She would get right to it.

She would take me and her family would take the boy's. They were too young to stay home alone. I knew they were in the best of hands and that was a relief for me. Every time I got back they would ask, "Are you okay now mama?"

My kids knew at a very young age what it was to worry. I hate knowing that but, not too much got passed my kids. If I could give my kids something back, it would be laughter. They cried along with me, and it broke my heart that they understood my pain. They would comfort me any way they could. They did little things to make me happy. As they got a little older, let me just put it this way, we kind of lived a backwards life. I was supposed to give them my undivided attention but they gave me their attention.

All medicine bottles say, "Keep out of reach of children." In my case I had to teach them how to open them for me but, how not to ever take one because it was for my pain. So it was never kept away from them. My medicine bottles were part of their life. They knew which one to give me in the morning, and how many. They know the colors and which day. They made a little stand just for my medicine bottles, so there wouldn't be any drama in the morning or at night when I got home. Talk about hot patches, knee brace, ankle brace, and wrist brace for carpel tunnel pain, you name it, I had it. Yes, it makes me feel guilty and I am one to want to ask questions. To? Why? Why couldn't this happen to me later in life when my kids were grown. No, they were so young. They would see me do something then they would catch on.

When I tried to open something Tommy would say, "Give it to me mama, I'll do it."

I spent a week at home because of the swelling and pain. My medicine was fighting against that concrete floor. If I didn't have to be on that concrete things would be better, but I had to be on it. That week, my kids organized the house for me.

James would say, "I'm putting this chair here with a pillow okay? Prop your leg on it so you can stretch okay mama."

Then Tommy asked, "Did you see where I put your water, it's there, don't get up. I will text and check on you"

Now I think about it and it's unbelievable to me how they helped me. I had to renew their medical insurance one day, me and James were home, even though Tommy helped me a lot I couldn't let that kid go anywhere because he would end up somewhere else. So I grounded him a lot. This time for some strange reason I let him go.

I said, "One and a half hours Tommy, that's it."

He replied with his, "Okay mama."

Two hours, three hours, four hours now I can't find him. I start calling the other mothers. "Have you seen Tommy around there?"

"No, not today."

"Okay, thanks." No one had seen him.

The phone rang and an unknown number showed up. "Hi mom, I know your mad but listen, I came to a party but the mom said she knew you from high school, and I'm with her son."

"Where?!"

"Oh like 9 miles, but don't worry were almost leaving."

James was the one gone a lot but he looked at me, "when is he coming back?"

"Soon!"

"Well okay it's that I needed to leave." James bluntly stated.

Shocked, I asked, "Where to? It's getting dark and your seven years old, where are you going?"

"Just up the street, I have been here with you all day already. Now its Tommy's turn"

"James you're lazy, go to bed. I'm not going to ask you for anything."

My kids knew so much about me that I would be sitting on my bed watching T.V. and they would run fast and jump on the bed and stop like an inch away from me. I would be saying "my knee, my knee."

"We know mom we're not going to hit you."

When they were boxing we would be at home I would leave one room and they would be going in and they would swing at me and I just closed my eyes. "Mom, you really think I was going to punch you?" They would get so close. The only time they hurt me was if they slept with me and they would sleep hard, they moved a lot especially James. He would stretch his leg and push my bad leg across the bed. You talk about pain, but he didn't know. What was strange about it was when he woke up and I was in bed awake,

he would look at me and with a low voice he would ask. "Did I hurt your leg mama? Are you mad?"

"No baby, I just had a bad night." One day when I got home from work the house was cold but Tommy knew how to turn the heat on.

I got off late and was going to be back there first thing the next morning. I was mad; it was so cold out there. I said, "Tommy why is the heat off? It's going to take a while to warm up, my legs are freezing!"

"Sorry mom, we were playing football."

I turned on some heat, was getting into bed and both of them jump on the bed had a couple more pillows the way I like, they got on each side of me with extra blankets, James threw his legs over mine for a little while, we laughed and cuddled and I slept like a baby. So warm, my legs didn't hurt in the morning and there was no stiffness.

When I woke up I knew they had given me their body heat and I just prayed to God and thanked him for the boys. I let them know, I said, "Thank you boys. I slept so well with no pain because of ya'll." That made them very happy.

We went through a lot of pain together. Sometimes I don't want to feel bad for them, but instead be thankful for the little helpers God gave me. Believe me when I say I am very thankful for what I have. I may not be surrounded by luxury items but the love and support I have from so many people and God is worth more than luxury to me.

Cold Weather

I n Texas it's very true when they say, "If you don't like the weather, just wait a little and it will change."

When I would go in early like 6:30 and it would be winter time, it could be 50 or 60 degrees in the morning. Then there were days when I walked outside and I would not expect for there to be ice on my windshield but there was. I would go back inside, get some water, my ice scraper and start scrapping the ice off.

"Mom, what are you doing?" the boys asked.

"I can't leave yet, there's ice on the car."

Having to scrape ice off the windshield was painful for my shoulders because it was early and cold. I had to stretch my arm across the windshield and then do the other side using my other arm. I can only describe it by saying a stabbing pain, just a very sharp pain in both shoulders. Sometimes I would even laugh because I would be scraping with my eyes closed. I just think it helped ease the pain a little. Maybe it didn't but I still closed them. I know I probably look dumb, that's why I laughed even if it was hurting.

One morning I was about to leave, I could not find my jacket. Good gosh what else! My Tommy has always worn big shirts, big pants, and big jackets. NO, I didn't like that at all. He gets up and hands me his jacket. He said "Just take my jacket mom, it should fit you." Really Tommy? Well I didn't argue with him he was putting it in my hands telling me to wear it. I told him I would wear it so I put the jacket on. I had to keep from laughing. You could see both my wrists and of course it did not close from the front but I wore it. I had tears in my eyes. I was laughing so hard on my way to work. Gotta love em!

After that happened a couple more times they would take turns going outside in the cold weather early in the morning to start my car for me so that I would not run late and so I could go straight into a warm car. I worried too, because at that time someone could have approached them. I would move the curtain aside to keep an eye out for them while I did my hair or whatever I was going to do. If I was going to go in at 6:30 meant one of them would be out there in the 5 a.m. hour. My children know I never MADE them do anything; they are the only ones (and God) that know what went on with me, like they say behind closed doors. The pain they saw me in, my reaction to sudden pain, the tears that came down my face just trying to get out of bed and taking them first few steps in the morning.

If it was a really bad night they would ask me if I was ready to go to bed, I would say yes. If I was watching T.V. in the living room they would help me to the bed, I would sit down and they would pick my legs up to the bed. Writing this book let me tell you, opened up a lot of closed wounds. My kids tell me that they remember most of what I have written and they say they can't believe that I actually made it through these years and I'm still working, still standing up all day long. If I sit them down and read part of a paragraph to them they start remembering and they get very emotional. Tommy did more and remembers more but that's because he is older and he wanted to do more for me. James is almost 2 years younger. He remembers a lot but didn't volunteer as much as Tommy did. But James is different, he wanted to play and color. That's what was on his mind and that's okay. I would get the unexpected from him. James was funny, he made me laugh a lot and that's good for the soul. Its little things like that that keeps you going.

A Backwards Phase

I remember the summer when I was able to start leaving them home alone. Oh I loved it, no more babysitters. When I would leave to work in the morning, James would walk me to the car every morning. I thought that was so cute. I would drive to the stop sign and I would look back and he would be standing on the porch waving at me.

Now Tommy is doing a few things that I didn't like. I talked to him about it and things didn't change. So I made arrangements with my mom, and soon Tommy would spent the rest of the summer at my mom's while I worked, then I would go by and pick him up. James followed all my rules, so he got to stay home. People could not understand why I would let the younger one stay home alone and not the older one. I thought it was funny. I just didn't trust Tommy.

My friends at work would hear me in the break room calling two places to check on them. Number one they couldn't understand why the oldest one went to my mom's or Ivan's moms and James was at the house. I explained to them why, but that's just how that summer went.

Tommy didn't fuss in the morning, he knew he was going and James was staying. James did follow all of my rules. Even during the year I let James play afterschool every day and Tommy had to go straight to my mom's house. Yes, I know it sounds unfair but Tommy knows exactly why he had to do that. Then I would go by my mom's and pick him up. My mom would let him go the park across the street or to his cousins for a little while. So that's my backwards story about the little one getting to stay home alone and the older one going to a sitter.

Strange but it worked. He would get mad if I told him to go to his friends for only 1 ½ hours. "That's for babies," he would say. He wanted 3 hours.

Well when he was with my mom he asked to go somewhere and she said okay, "But only for 20 minutes" He wanted to faint when she said that and he couldn't wait to tell me. Me and the boys have had good days and bad days and really bad days together. Some days they would understand me and some days they just didn't want to hear me. They think I should have had them at 19 and 20 years old. Then I would be a cool mom, but I had them later and now I'm just an old fashioned mom. They know I love them and I know they love me but, thank God I was a poor girl with 3 T.Vs. There were days when we would each go to a room, close the door and watch our own movie and get passed our feelings. Then there were days when we watched the same T.V and had a great time. I always told my kids Mama is Mama, Mama is not your friend. That may sound strange also, but I have my friends. I will not be my child's best friend that could cause problems. I don't want them to treat me like they do their friends, that is not what I'm here for.

They get it now, but they thought I was rude at first. Some families do see their kids as their friend and that's all good. It's just not for me. My mom is my mom and that's how I see her. I love and respect my parents but we don't see each other as friends. I'm a very friendly person, I have a lot of them but it's just not my kids. We joke around a lot and laugh together. I think I'm a very sassy mother with my kids but to me when all this is happening I consider it good family time. My kids do not understand my rules. They are not very difficult but they are old fashioned and that's where we clash! It was easier when they were younger. Now we just can't seem to get on the same page about some things but, were working on it. They love to spend the night at friend's houses, I'm against it. They need to know where home is every night. I tell them everyone should go home at night. Go back the next day but, learn how to be home every night. I just think those are good family values that will hopefully help them one day when their older. That's normally when they do get what you say. Sadly until then they just think were picking on them.

At least my kids think that. Just like the being friends relationship. No, I had to stop them from telling me I was trippin, or to chill out. I don't like any of that. If I call them on the cell, I want a hello. Tommy answers and says, "Yo".

See those are all the things he can tell his friends, not his mother. They both have gotten better at not talking to me like that. They just don't see where they are disrespecting me. That kind of talk to me is disrespectful. One day the boy's call me at work. Tommy is on the line.

"Hello?"

"Mom its Tommy, can me and James go to a party?"

"No." I reply, "I'm not getting off until closing time, and I don't know where you will be, whose party? Plus I don't know who the parents are."

"You never let us go anywhere."

He hangs up on me. Ten minutes later I get another call. It's Tommy again.

"Please mom, can we go?"

"Tommy parties can be dangerous and . . ." but then he interrupts me.

"Well you just use us, I'm tired of helping you. I have wanted to tell you that for a long time now that we're tired of it. Both of us are.

Just start doing everything yourself. Don't ask us anymore." Then he hangs-up.

I have to go back to the register and work and pretend everything's okay. That was very hard to hear. I took a little break, went to the ladies room and of course I silently cried, then I have to get myself together to go get back on the register. Tough. If that's what's was in his heart, he sure got it out. I got home that night and they are asleep. I went to give them a kiss. I went straight to bed and morning came quick. Tommy wakes up and goes to my room. Tommy said with a shaky voice, "Mama, are you awake?"

"Yes son I have to leave pretty soon"

"Mama, please don't go to work today. Me and James don't want to go to school, just be with us. Call your manager. Can you?" he then continues to say, "Mom, I'm sorry for what I said last night, I didn't mean it and you know I didn't." James was just standing behind him with tears running down his face.

"Mama, I made you a salad last night, did you eat it?" asks James.

I answer, "No baby I didn't see it, I just went straight to bed."

I know that deep inside we were missing each other. We were living under the same roof, but it can happen. I started making Sundays even more special. I prepared their favorite meals, we set the table up and we (like always) prayed over our food. It gave us family time and they were able to tell me about their days at school. James is still hoping I can one day be that stay at home mom that he has always wanted.

"I just want you to make me some *sopita* after school." James says.

I did make it all the time but he had to warm it up, because I wasn't there. He said it wasn't the same. On my days off I would prepare a big breakfast and a great after school meal. I looked forward to these days because they took my days off even more serious than me. If sitting at a table with food can make your family happy and a good conversation to catch up on what's been going on, than do it. I found out how simple things can make a family grow closer. It doesn't cost a penny.

Giving

My boys are very giving boys. Ever since Tommy was a very young boy he wondered why people would walk around.

He spoke very clear "Why he's walking around?"

"Don't know baby"

"Oh," He would just stare at them.

When he was about 5, boy did he want to know where they were going. "Are they hot or are they cold?" To me it was hard to explain to a 5 year old what a homeless person was. As months went by I explained a little bit to him. They don't have money, and they don't have a house to sleep in.

"Oh, well why not?"

Then one day we were out and he said, "I'm hungry." I got him a little happy meal.

"Stop mama, stop!" He exclaimed.

"What?! Why?!" I asked startled.

"Look he is hungry, I'm gonna give him my food."

I froze. I said, "Really and you're not going to cry?"

"No."

So I go around, stop and give him the happy meal. We take off and Tommy starts laughing and waving at him. He, to this day has always been giving food to the homeless. James is the same way. You just don't know how many times we have told a homeless person, "Just stay right there, don't leave. We're going to get you something to eat".

After we do that they are so happy that someone is not hungry. James will draw shelters with beds and all. He said, "Mom, when I grow up I'm gonna make this for the homeless". They need a place to sleep. They collect shoes and we take them to churches where they give them out. When they were in 3rd and 4th grade they took cans every day during the holidays. They would put them in their backpacks. I noticed our pantry was looking a little empty. I said, "Where are my cans?"

Tommy answered, "In school, people need to eat so I took them"

"Me too mama, people are hungry," James said in a serious tone.

A Church Downtown

I met 2 young ladies at my job who work for a church. They buy groceries there at my job. One day I was in the store shopping with my boys and I introduced them to the two ladies. Later that day my kids asked me about the children. I said well they don't have regular homes or they no longer have parents.

"Why?" They both asked.

Good question. "I'm not too sure."

My kids asked me a puzzling question, "Mom, do the kids go to parties,? Do they ever get a candy bag?" It stayed on my mind for days.

The next time I saw them in the store I asked them if it would be okay to make candy bags for the kids. They said yes. Oh my kids were so happy to hear that. That next year we made candy bags, about ten bags once a week (pretty ones) and I would take them to work and the girls would pick them up. Then the children would make a big thank you card for the boys. It was a lot of fun they really enjoyed that.

My kids love to feed people. I told my mom one day, "Mom, I'm about to blind fold your grandson."

"*Por que?*(Why?)"

I said, "He can spot a homeless person a mile away! He was about 7 when we were driving down the road."

He said, "There he is. Hey there he is"

"Who?" I thought for a moment and I had seen a man waiting for the city bus.

"Yes mama that's him, he's hungry."

I said, "Well I can't stop in this traffic son. I don't know what to do."

"He needs food."

It was so difficult to explain to a 7 year old that we cannot get to everyone.

I was watching television one day when they both ran in very red in the face. First thing Tommy says, "Mama, can you make 40 enchiladas please. Just make 40 enchiladas. I looked at him and he said, "My friend knows some people that are hungry.

James stands behind him saying, "Yes they're hungry."

So I asked his friends and he said it was some people that lived down the street from him. I was never able to speak to an adult so I really didn't know if they were homeless or hungry.

I have a sister in law who has a grandson that needs a liver transplant. A couple years back he had been in and out of the hospital, so I decided to check on him. When I called there was no answer so I decided to call my mother and I asked her if she heard anything. As she gave me notice and we exchanged information back and forth. Tommy comes into the room. My sister in laws grandson was about 5 at the time. Tommy was half asleep, it was around 7 a.m.

"Mom, who are you talking to? Whoever it is, tell him I will give him my liver," he continued, "Please mom I want to help him. Please can I?"

I told my mom what Tommy said. Deep in our hearts we knew he couldn't be the one, but my mom told me to call my sister in law and let Tommy talk to her. Thankfully she answered and Tommy started talking to her, she also knew he couldn't help but for him to think of that was just incredible.

I could hear her talking to him saying, "Thank you Tommy that means so much to me, I will never forget that." After taking him on a cruise for his 10th birthday, he wanted a party, I said no. I already took you on a cruise. We argued about having a party for about a week, I finally gave in. I said "Okay Tommy I will make you a party."

My friend that went with us on the cruise received notice a week later that she had cancer. I felt really bad for her. I was telling the boy's because they really like her. The next morning Tommy told me he no longer wanted a party he just wanted to donate his birthday money to a cancer patient, to my friend. We ended up raising a lot of money for her, including where we work.

A Better Offer

I started working at the warehouse March 11, 2003. I remember I was part time closing every night I worked. Things seemed to be going my way. After a few weeks of the night shift my manager asked if I wanted to pick up a different shift. She said a lady was having a baby and she needed someone to replace her. I immediately said okay, now I'm working days. After a couple of months she moved to another store. Before she left she told me she would be making me a fulltime employee. Great, more money. I took that too. She said, "What days would you like to be off?" I said well not sure but at least Sundays.

I wanted to have a full day with my kids. So now I need one more day because I need to be off 2 days. It was back and forth from Tuesday to Thursdays. For sure I had off my Sundays. I remember reading the bible on how it was at the beginning and how God created the earth, and on the seventh day he rested. I know I'm not God, but I think everyone should be off on Sundays. "Thank you God." I have seen so many cashiers come and go, all part time. I have been the only full time cashier for a long time now. (For years) I think she was there to give me the job, get me day hours, and make me full time. Soon after, she was gone to another store. It's been a couple of years since I've seen her.

A Part Time Job

My friend told me about a flea market that had a lot of business over the weekend. I thought to get ahead a part time job sounded well, but I knew I needed one where I could take my kids with me. The flea market sounded good. I bought a popcorn machine at work, made my arrangements at the flea market and now I have a part time job. I would go there Saturday mornings and set up and work half a day then pack up and go to my ware house job. I get off at night and back to the flea market early on Sunday morning. That went on for about 2 years. It wasn't all year I only did it in the summer and part of the fall. There were times when it got dangerous; I would work the food side during the day. Then at night there would be dancing and that took part in the back part of the flea market. The music was for all ages, families with kids or just single grown people. Some people got drunk and there would be fights that broke out every now and then. Police out there would help me out by watching my kids.

They were doing their job, but they just helped me out by keeping an eye on them. Fall finally came and the owner said tomorrow is going to be a cold day but it should be a good day in sales, so just get ready. I said okay. Tommy was not feeling well so I left him with my mom. James cried and didn't want to stay, so, I took him, things were in full swing, when James raised his arms for me to pick him up, I got a chair and carried him, rubbed his back for a little while and he was out for the night. One of the police officers scooted over a picnic table that was not being used and I wrapped him up in blankets and laid him down on the picnic table next to me. I felt bad and sad because it was so cold but I finished the night. Back to work at the warehouse on Monday and then just repeated that pattern over and over again. It did help me get ahead because I was trying to save some money to get a place of my own.

I rented a house in the north side area of Fort Worth in February 2004. I'm still living there. I know that nobody loves their landlord, {laughing} but I do, I have the best landlord, I love him. I wanted to stay in the same place while my children were in elementary school. I think it's a bad idea when people keep moving their kids around, different address, enrolling them in a new school all the time. I know, just like I stayed in different houses. Yes people sometimes don't have a choice but to keep moving. I feel like that was another goal I accomplished, keeping the same address.

Personal Help

The way my boys started helping me so much (I think) is they saw how I struggled to put on socks, and tie my shoes. I cried everyday as I was getting dressed, "Here mama, I will help you." They did my socks, then each one did a tennis shoe and tied them. More knots than anyone could count but hey, they were tied. They saw it was less pain for me. From then on they helped me with my shoes and socks. Soon it seemed like they were dressing me.

As they were helping me I would tell them, "One day I will reward you." Never a response. Rainy days were torture, my shoulders would get so stiff, not even medicine or a hot shower worked. I was almost dressed, BOOM. I could not put my shirt on. James saw me and said look mom give me both of your arms. So I reached my arms out to him and he would do circular motions, it would hurt but they did warm up. When he was moving my arms, a big tear fell to the floor, I saw it fall, I looked at him and he turned. That was enough for me to get all the strength I needed.

I said, "I'm good baby, I think I can get my arms through the sleeves now."

"No! I got it mom."

He gets my work shirt, puts it over my head then he helps me with the sleeves. All very slowly. As he is helping me, I'm asking God in my mind, *"Why?"* Then I think, well if I'm the chosen one, there's nothing I can do. You certainly can't pass it to someone else and say, "Here it's your turn". I wish it was that easy. So now, there's nothing else to ask. I know I have arthritis, but I also know that God gave me a powerful mind. I put it to work, and try to figure out what I can do to help better myself. I do buy a lot of health magazines on arthritis; I read everything I can just to educate myself more about it. As a family I see us all going through it. I feel bad, because my kids were so young at the time. The pain sometimes was way more than I could handle.

There were 2 things that really helped me, ice and elevating my leg. I didn't use a cold patch or even bags. Sometimes I would just get big pieces of ice and just set them on my knee. The cold didn't bother me. I would sit on my bed, get a big thick towel, and fold it in half and put it under my knee. Then rub the ice on it. It was also free medicine, because it did help. Sometimes I would feel so sad. I would think, is this a test from God? maybe! He gave me my job, I know he did, but he never said it would be easy. I have worked there almost 10 years and 9 out them have been in pain. All the customers know.

Everybody knows. My co-workers and customers have been more than wonderful to me. Customers ask me daily how I'm doing. It makes me feel real good to know that people care. We have a pharmacy in the store. The pharmacy employees have done so much for me. They have filled my prescriptions for years. Even though the pharmacist likes to pretend he doesn't know me when I show up there. Another one of the ladies always tells me they cannot fill an order or give me the amount I want.

I say, "Okay, well thank you."

She says, "Not really, I'm just joking!" I fall for it every time. She sounds so serious.

They are all wonderful people. If I'm working and I'm out of medication, I will ask anyone of them that passes by and they will gladly help me. One lady just knows all my information, she tells me what I have, how much I have left and what she can do to get me by the day. They call the doctor for me, I just love them all. Another one of the ladies always asks me how I'm doing. She knows that me and her hurt on the same days. I'm very thankful to have the help I need right there where I work.

I'm very thankful to my two nephews. They will also do whatever they can, whenever they can. I'm truly blessed to have great people around me. One day my two nephews watched my kids over the weekend. One of them called me and I missed the call because I was working, but I called back on my break.

He said, "We are back from out of town I will drop them off at your job so that you don't have to come all the way over here."

"No problem sounds good!"

He dropped them off I gave them money for pizza they sat at a table near my register. I turned to tell them something and they were now giving me their back. Didn't think much about it, when I left to go clock out Tommy waves at me, saying, "Mom I'm sorry we turned we just couldn't stand to see you move that heavy stuff so we just turned around."

I just said, "It's okay baby, I'm done for today."

Things were heavy, but if you just ask God to give you the strength that you need every day he will give it to you. I thank him all day long any chance I get. Retail can be very tough, but if you can just stay focused on the positive you will have a good out come at the end of the day. It's not always easy but just stay focused.

Putting my personal life aside

When I became a single mother I had a three year old and a five year old. I knew I wanted to do the best job I could as a single mother with the 2 kids I had. I knew from the very beginning that I didn't want to have any more children and one thing I knew for sure was that I did not want a step father for my kids. All I wanted was to respect them and I wanted them to know I would always be there for them and that no man would ever come between us. I have known of very good stepfathers, but I have also known of really bad ones. I just chose not to do that to my kids.

Not only that, I did not have it in my heart to let my kids see me in bed with a man. By that I mean I did not want my kids to go into my room when they woke up or me to go to bed first and then they go to me for whatever reason and see me. Not in a bad way. If you're in a relationship and you decide to move in together, than more than likely you will share a room together. Well, kids go in to their parents' bedroom to wake them up if they are hungry or if they get scared.

It could be any reason, that's what I couldn't get passed. I just never wanted my kids to see me in bed with a man.

I never invited any man just to come over and hang out with me and the boys. It could also be a mistake, but it's too late. I already did it this way. I was done with the fighting and the arguing, and all the stress that comes with that. That didn't mean no one ever came over when they were in school or when they went out of town for the weekend. As long my kids weren't around everything was okay. I had a couple of dinner dates, movie dates or I would go to a cook out when I was invited, but all this was later. Nothing at the beginning. After all I am human.

The boys were about 8 and 10 years of age, when they came up to me and said boyfriends were bad. Tommy starts crying a little and says, "Mom, don't have a boyfriend they are going to hurt your feelings."

James says, "Oh yes and if anyone ever hurts you they are going to be sorry." They are very protective of me now, so this does go back to when they were younger also.

"Tommy said, "They just want to get fresh."

I just turned around and laughed. I said, "Okay boy's time for bed."

Now it's a little hard to have a relationship, where I think I might introduce someone to the boys. They are in no hurry for that. Then for a long time I know I was in no condition to be in a relationship. The concrete floor at work has a lot to do with it. It's tough, I use a good mat but I'm not on that mat all day. I just don't think it's fair to a good looking man, that's what I'm thinking. It's because I limp, I'm uncomfortable with that. I am better now, but I still limp a little. I will say one thing, I'm tired of it. I told myself I would better myself. It's painful, and will exhaust you.

My boys have grown up taking care of me. That's also not fair to them. One day James got on a chair to get me some water; he was about 6 years old. He took a long time to come back to the room.

Finally he came in and gave me my water and said, "Look mom, come look at what I did" He had a funny look on his face.

I thought, "oh no, there was no telling what I was going to see." I got up, went to the kitchen and he had filled up about 7 or 8 disposable cups of water I mean full was not the word. My jaw dropped! He looked at me with that smile, "See mama, it's for you, for your arthur-ritis." (that's how they pronounced it) I just think he was trying to make things easy on me. I guess in case I needed water, it was already made for me. I did love things like that. They made me laugh and it cheered me up.

I didn't know I was doing all the wrong things. I should have been stretching and walking more. I tried getting up extra early so that the kids would not see me get up. I held on to the bed, then I would hold on to the wall. The wall was my guide to get to the little hall way. I had no choice I had to moan, the pain was a stabbing pain. Sometimes the boys would wake up.

Quietly in a low voice Tommy says, "Mom, I will help you to the shower."

"No baby just stay in bed, I'm almost there." I was crying of course.

"Okay Mom," he said in a very shaky voice, "but if you need me, just call me. I'm gonna stay awake."

It just killed me to hear that. I would get in the hot shower and just cry. I would cry for my pain and my baby's pain.

One day I got out of the shower Tommy was awake and had a very happy voice. I said, "Son, what are you doing up already?"

He said, "Look, sit right here." He had folded a towel into a square and put it on his bed. He got a second towel and folded that one the same way and put it on the floor. One towel was for me to sit on and the second one was for my feet.

So I did what he wanted me to and he said, "Are you better now? Does that feel good to your arthur-ritis?"

Those were the times, I just wanted to "explode" trying to smile and make my kids happy by saying yes, but I was holding back a hard cry. My heart couldn't take it anymore. I assured him that what he did had made my day and that it did make my arthritis better.

My job is very physical, but on top of that it had become very stressful. It's like I say I'm a single mother raising two boys. Very deep down inside, I felt depressed. Depressed because a lot of the times I could not express to anyone the way I was feeling. I had to hide it at work, I didn't want to always be telling the kids I didn't feel good. So with them I pretended I wasn't hurting, but I was. I didn't want to stress or worry my parents so I didn't say much about it to them. I had to continue to put on faces for everybody.

Later there was no hiding it at my job anymore. People could tell I was hurting. They asked me all the time. They showed a lot of concern and helped me a lot. My job has been good to me and my kids. I have been able to live alone with them. I have been able to take them on beautiful vacations, provide for them and so much more. I do still hurt a little at work, but not near as much as I use to. I just take my medicine and continue to take one day at a time. When I was taking over the counter medicine, I had hope back then that it would take care of my problem.

Thinking that one day, I'm just going to wake up and my pain is gonna be no more. Well, that was not the case here. My sister told me to enroll in the country hospital. She said they have a good arthritis specialist. So I did. It was a very long process, and a very long wait being it was the county hospital. I waited and waited and waited my turn. I tried to be patient. Finally in 2010 I got medical treatment. The treatment mellowed the pain. It was better than the job I was doing on my own. When I was taking care of it myself I would take 5 over the counter pills in the morning, 2 at noon and 5 more at night. 84 pills a week for about 3 weeks. Yes I know, stupid. I'm surprised I'm not dead. The good Lord knows I was just trying to keep doing my job and that was to provide for my kids.

Two strong boys

Blessed is the word to use when it comes to my boys. When I was at my worst, even though we all three lived together, I still tried to hide some of my pain from my children but there were days especially nights, when it was impossible to hide my pain.

My boys would bring me my medicine, and would ask, "What can I do for you mom?" They rubbed my back and sat by me. If I ran out of hot patches and wraps they would find anything and would cut anything in long strips just to wrap around my knee to keep it tight. One day I woke up with 2 bandanas tied together just to get it around my swollen knee, but I have to say it did make me laugh.

We had our way of doing things, getting on my bed was painful. I had to sit down. I had a little tiny bench by my bed that I would put my feet on, and then the boys would help me lift my leg very slowly on to the bed. You would think I was about to get some relief by going to bed but it was a bad time. Relaxing brought on pain for me. Moving or turning was the worst pain ever. Mornings came really quick. I took an extra hour and a half just to walk slow and warm up. I did a lot of crying, but crying also helped me. I just wish I could have hid that crying face more.

Now that my boys are older they help me with a lot of home therapy. Arthritis seems to be mellowing a little; you just have to learn to control it. I'm just amazed at all the things they have done for me. The younger one, James, became even more concerned, as where Tommy had already been doing a lot for me.

Then my hands started with the same symptoms. Aching, stiff and started to make things difficult for me. In a way, that was bringing me down again. It got in my way of driving, I couldn't turn it was a stabbing pain. So getting out of my drive way, I would back out on to the street and whichever boy was sitting up front would turn the wheel for me. If I got to a stop sign and then had to make a left or right turn, they would help me turn the wheel. As I drove, one day we laughed and I said nobody can possibly be doing the same thing we are.

This is absolutely crazy, but we were laughing. Who helps their mom turn the steering wheel? Sometimes you just have to look over that gray cloud and really laugh. My kids get embarrassed when I laugh loud at a restaurant. They say, "Mom, sshh please." They do say it's better than seeing me in pain. They absolutely hate to see me in pain, but what do we do? Have faith and keep going.

At one time the inflammation was so bad and so painful that I had to be off work, I will never forget April 24, 2010 to May 25, 2010. Right before that I went to so many emergency rooms. When I say it got bad believe me, that's when I really thought arthritis had taken over me. I didn't know what else to do. I didn't know how to keep it under control. I thought I had tried everything. What do I do? I think about my kids and I know they need me. My shoulders bothered me but not as much as my knee. This time it was the back of my knee. The worst pain, it felt like a pinched nerve.

I cried before I went to work. I got to work and pretended to be okay. When my shift was over, I would get in my car and just cry. Then I would clean my face before I got home so that the boys would not question me. Quitting my job was out of the question. I was just not going to do that. I would just think, "I have two babies," repeatedly in my head and it was my job to provide.

Our bedrooms are right next door to each other. One night I took my pills, my younger son James saw me take them. I closed the door between us because I didn't want to hear the T.V. He opened it. I closed it again. I'll be damned he opened it. I waited a few minutes. I closed it again. I got in bed and he opened it again, but pushed it open with an angry look. Before I could say anything he looked right into my eyes.

The look on his face was like nothing I had seen before, and he said in a strong tone, "Don't close it Mom. If you close it, I'm afraid I will open it later and you might be dead."

Then he just hugged me for a long time and I always assured them that no matter how sick I got, I would do whatever it took not to leave this earth and leave them without a mom.

Another day he shocked me by being awake early in the morning unexpectedly. I remember him saying good night from his room. I yelled, "Good night," back.

Then it seemed liked only minutes when James wakes me up. He is on my bed sitting at my feet. This is about 3 a.m. When I opened my eyes I looked at him and he had my leg on his leg and he was rubbing my knee and said, "Wake up Mom, you're in pain, what can I get you?" It sounded like he wanted to cry. I just started crying and told him how much I loved him and thanked him for waking me up. I told him that alone made me feel better. He stayed next to me for a couple of hours and then went back to his room.

Tommy got home from school one day and said, "Mom I need to talk to you. Have you been feeling okay, because I noticed you have been resting a lot."

I said, "I'm just resting when I can, I hurt a little but don't worry."

He said, "Mom, it hurts me so bad to see you hurting. I want to make things easier for you. I think about you in school. I wonder if you're okay, if you're having a good day at work, and praying that people help you move heavy things."

Hearing him say that made me feel good, but then again I thought, "Heck no! I have to do more walking, more home therapy. I don't want them to think that way. Especially in school, I don't want my illness to get in the way of their studies." I talked to him and politely told him he did not have to think about me in school. If something was wrong he would know before he went to school.

They went through a lot with me. James handles it in a different way. He is stronger and more straightforward with me. He tells me "Mom did you take your joint juice? Tell me the truth" or "Here is your medication, take it in front of me"

Sometimes I have my glass of water but before I warm up, picking up a glass of water is too painful. So I keep telling myself over and over, "I'm fixing to take it."

James comes back in the room and says, "Take it mom, it could have already started working for you, but your taking too long."

If there is something is that is going to make me faster, and make me feel like a perfectly healthy woman it would most definitely be a dog running towards me. I'm so scared of dogs. Since I've had arthritis, my mom's dog came at me. A stray dog at the gas station, and some Chihuahuas that the neighbors down the street own. You think I wont forget all about my arthritis and do the hundred yard dash but, yes I will. I don't care who is around, I'm running.

One day I looked like a criminal. I got out of my car to get gas; I went around my car and never saw the big dog that was next to the pump. When I saw it, I ran across the parking lot. I was looking at the cashiers as I ran. Then I pushed the door open, and ran in the store. I think he must have thought I had a gun and was fixing to rob the store, I don't know. All I know is that I ran. No pain, no nothing. When I was inside the attendant said, "Ma'am, that dog was never behind you." I don't care, but it did look at me. That's why I ran. I don't always want to get chased by dogs.

Home therapy is good enough for me. My nights are 90% better; it's a blessing to be able to say that. When it was time to get up and get ready for work, I did what I could, then they would help me. I would put my shoes on, that was painful to do. They would help me tie them because my fingers wouldn't bend that way, they wouldn't because of the stiffness. Then I would put my jeans on and lay on the bed so that Tommy could button and zip them. I was embarrassed to ask them if they could help me with my button and zipper at first. Now I can do it, I just have days when I do need help like rainy cloudy days.

Now when they have to help me, it's so natural. It's just faster and easier. When we are at a restaurant they know I have to get up first, they stay sitting down. That's because it gives me time to stand up and warm up, and then when they get up we just all start walking. We have a pattern down. They have learned about arthritis so well. Sometimes they get on the computer and start looking up things that can help me. If I'm reading they will come into my room and tell me, "Guess what I just found out," then they will explain to me what they found. I thank them all the time for everything that they have done for me. I thank God for giving me my boys.

My sweet little Tommy would yell from another room, "Anything you need Mom just call me." I hardly heard that from James, but it was okay. He would do anything for me when I asked. Arthritis pain would do whatever it wanted to do whenever it wanted to. Some days I could handle it. Then there were crying pain days.

One day I was running later for work a big no-no for me. My wrist was killing me and I couldn't my brush hair. Tommy said, "Mom, let me do it. Do I just brush down over and over."

I just said, "Do whatever you want to do baby." I wore a pony tail every day. So getting a band around my thick hair was a job in itself and I had to do it. I always cried after I dropped them off at school. It just saddened me to know that I couldn't do those things for myself. I bought a stress ball for my hands. I will squeeze it when I'm watching T.V. or just any chance I get, and it has helped strengthen my hands.

My Lowest Arthritis Moment

One morning I was getting ready for work. We didn't have much of a winter this year, but then there were cool days that bothered me, some more than others. I was almost ready and I was putting on my bra, which had tiny clips on the front. I put it on started clipping that first one and I felt a crippling pain. I just took a deep breath and clipped together a second one, and again a pain so tremendous. I was trying to cry softly but nothing gets past Tommy.

He heard me, taps on the door and slowly opens it. I was sitting on the bed. I just had to sit there for a few minutes and let the pain go away. Then Tommy just walks right in and says "Mom I know something is wrong, don't tell me everything is okay. What is it?"

He was already in tears. I quickly covered myself with my shirt and he said, "Tell me, are you hurting it's okay, I'll help you."

I just laid back, put the shirt over my face and just cried as loud as I could. I thought, "No way! No way! This will not take over me!" But at the moment it did. The pain did take over me.

Tommy hugged me and said, "It's going to be alright mom, you know why? God gave you <u>me</u> for a reason, it's okay. Let me help you."

That was the lowest point of my arthritis life, my son helping me with my bra. I will win this battle, now I'm more determined than ever to do something about it. Determination can change a lot of things. It can make a huge difference in your life, all because one chose to be determined. We can get out of any situation if we set our minds to it. Our minds are very powerful. Don't ever give up. A bad situation is not impossible to turn around. Try it.

A Close Call

When I lived with my mom after separating from my kid's dad, I didn't have a job or money. I helped her a lot around the house, I cleaned. If she had to go anywhere I would tell her to go do what she needed and I would do what she had to do at home. I also helped her make tamales. She made them during the holidays. That was a very busy time for her. I helped her so much that I learned how to make them on my own.

After I started working this lady asked me if I would make her some. So I did, a couple of days later people were asking me for more and more. I decided its a little extra money and I'm at home working where my kids are so, no problem. It was like a part time job. It became a lot of work for me. They are very time consuming. I was finishing up a batch when James comes in the kitchen and says,

"Mom, I need some new t-shirts and some more socks." He was in 5th grade. He had asked me to take him earlier in the week but I was too busy making tamales.

I figured I better make some time and take him. I said, "Okay, go get your shoes on and put on a jacket." Meanwhile I started cooking another batch. A lot of people do not like leaving their house when they have tamales on but I had to.

Not all the time but sometimes I had to leave and pick up the boys or just to my mom's house, not long at all. I start putting my water in, then I started lining up the tamales inside, I covered them. They don't require a lot of water only the bottom of the pot. I normally start by turning up the heat on high for about the first 5 to 7 minutes then I turn it back down on low and they steam cook. So we leave, I even went and picked up my sister and her son. We were having a great time. I picked up a few groceries while we were out and about. We were gone about an hour and half total time. That next batch was going to steam slowly about two hours. While we shopped it crossed my mind "Did I turn down the heat?" yes I did, but it still bothered me. If I did, I would clearly remember doing it. "Yeah it's okay, my neighbor would have already called."

After shopping my son said the famous words he and Tommy are famous for, "Mom, I'm hungry." So we stop at a restaurant and they were eating and laughing all of a sudden I didn't think things were very funny anymore. I said we have to go. I still have a lot to do. I remember thinking again if something would have happened; my neighbor would have called, okay so now I calm down a little. No, I kept thinking did I turn it down? I did, I didn't, I did, no, I'm going crazy.

I dropped my sister off and took off fast. I said "James, I don't remember If I turned the fire down."

He looked at me and said, "Oh no mom did you?" I still had hope because there was no phone call. I get a block away, I look up to the sky and I think, "Okay, no smoke, were good! I turn the corner and my neighbor across the street is having a huge cook out. A lot of people are there. I look at my house and think, oh thank you God. So we fly out of the car, I unlock the front door and when I opened it my house was filled with white smoke. James runs to the kitchen and at this point I no longer care if the house is burning. I just need to get James out, but I could barely see him. He said he ran because when he went inside you could see the very bright fire through the smoke. He turned it off as fast as he could. I thought my heart was going to pop out of my chest. I think okay the burner is off. All of this is my fault for rushing. I don't want to open the front door and ruin the cook out with fire trucks showing up. If I open it all the way too much smoke will come out. I will scare everyone. My neighbor's house faces the other direction so her backyard faces my front yard. Having fire trucks here will be major drama. We know we had it under control; we just needed a way to get the smoke out.

We open the back door and open the back windows. Thank God one window was already broken. When we were opening windows and the back door we are holding our breath. Smoke is now clearing. It is slowly escaping out the windows and the back door. We had to play it off. We go to the porch and sit on a bench we never use. Never! We were huffing and puffing our hearts were still racing. My son is light complected so his cheeks were very red. I'm not very light complected but I was pale at that moment. We were sitting there with the porch light on, but all the lights in the house were off. We were afraid people would see the smoke. Now it's more an embarrassment than anything else. Me and James are sitting on the porch outside, we look like two idiots.

Now my neighbor from across the street having the cook out sees us sitting there, waves at us and says "*Buenas noches*." Really! Nothing good over here, but we wave back like two dummies. We now look like we're desperate to get invited to the cook out. Finally it's clear enough for us to go inside. Now, time to take the burning pot to the backyard and take the lid off. My tamales looked crunchy. They were all still standing, because there is no room for them to lean, but tamales are not supposed to crunch.

We cleaned stuff up and went to spend the night at my parents' house; we could not stand the smell of burned tamales all night. Get ready for this; I hope your sitting down, the next week I did it again. Yep! Red flag. God is telling me to slow down. I picked up on that flag too. I said no more. How lucky can I be? I do count my blessings. I watch my kids and God watches me. Wow! What a close call. That's why I give thanks every day. To all the busy mom's and dad's out there, slow down. Do only what you can. Don't throw in extras because it may cost you. It almost cost me my house twice. That was a horrible feeling. Just be thankful for what you have. Remember your sanity comes first. Slow down and enjoy your kids. Life is too short and our kids grow up fast.

Driving

One day I felt so guilty, because at the time I was driving a huge van. Oh my gosh! My cars, that's a whole other story . . . but Tommy was 12 or 13 when I said, "Let's go get groceries."

It sounded good at the moment, but then pain hit and I could not even turn the keys. Tommy said, "Mom let me drive, it's a straight shot once we leave the driveway."

I sat there for a few minutes and thought about it. It wasn't like he was going by himself, but still it was a little scary. I knew I had to feed them. It wasn't a question of, if I should feed them. I said, "Okay Tommy, but do exactly what I tell you to do. No playing around."

I felt horrible. Like I said he was like 12 or 13 at the time, a little kid with a red and blue baseball cap driving this huge van. I prayed all the way to the grocery store. We got to the parking lot and he smiled from ear to ear and said, "See mom I told you I could." So after that, he was wanting to drive me around the neighborhood. To my mom's house about 4 blocks away, the gas station and of course the grocery store. Little by little they both started driving a little more and then bigger and busier streets. It was scary because they were so young but that little bit of driving they did at the driving park really helped. It happened to come in very handy. Tommy started looking into a driving permit when he turned 15. He just wanted to drive me around everywhere.

They told him he had to have a good reason to do that at 15. He never worried about that. He knew his reason was a good one. When they were ten and eleven I took them to a driving park, it was just turns and stops. It was next to a little river and there were trees and a baseball field to the other side. They loved it but I would only let them drive for 15 or 20 minutes each. Gas was too high, and that's how they got started.

Not long after that my younger one started telling me, "You never let me take you anywhere. Next time I want to drive to the grocery store."

So I let him and he did very well also, so now I have 2 chauffeurs. When it came to the pain we really risked it. We did get into small arguments in the car because they thought, I'm driving she's on the passenger side seat so I drive my way. No! Not at all. One day they will know what I meant by leave a car space between you and the car in front of you. I hope they remember everything I told them about all the responsibilities that come with driving. You drive; you are responsible for everyone in that car. Teaching young kids responsibilities seems like it will never work, but just keep talking to them, say it over and over whatever it is that you want them to know. They might get tired of you but sooner or later they will repeat what you have been drilling in their mind and that's a good thing.

Sports

Every day I thought, today cannot be about me, I have to do something. I remember my sister asking me if I would let James join their boxing team. She said her and her husband would be in charge of him. They had a son and daughter in boxing. I would be working the hours they had to be at the gym. I thought, "Oh, boxing I'm not sure."

So I said, "Let me think about it and I will let you know."

"Well, let me know as soon as possible, he is 8 years old and that's when they start."

A few days went by and I called her. I told her I had talk to James and he wanted to do it. I got him registered, and he started training and working out. So cute!

After a few weeks went by my sister said, "If you're off today, come by the gym so that you can watch them spar" I said okay. Well, I didn't think it was very cute when I saw him get hit. It took a while for me to get use to that. Soon they were both going. Tommy was 9. The boys wanted me to take them any chance I got instead of my sister.

So now I work, I volunteer at the school a little and not a soccer mom but just a sports mom.

The boys would tell me, "Mom I need different gloves" or "Mom, I want my own head gear" or "Boxing shoes and so on and so on."

One day I walked into the gym and the coach flags me down. He said either you stay home or you stay away from them. I was a little lost. I said okay I can go home but why are you telling me this? That's just the way he is, strict not in a bad way. He is a great coach.

He said, "Well first of all Tommy is the biggest mama's boy I know."

Now I'm not lost anymore. I got it real quick. He said, James will not work out unless his mat is right by your feet when you're here.

I'm not going to the gym as much, just dropping them off. If I did, I would stay far away or listen to the radio in the parking lot. Closer to the yearly boxing tournament, which takes place in February the coach would say, "Okay we're meeting in Grand Prairie tomorrow, be there by 5:30 p.m."

What! 5:30 p.m. I get off of work at 5. I have to count my money, go pick up the boys and where the f$!& is Grand Prairie? How will we get there in this traffic? How can I rush if I'm limping? Somehow we made it, a little late but we made it. The coach again says, "Okay guys tomorrow we meet at the gym in Irving at the same time."

Oh no! Both days were news to me. I work tomorrow night, and I close. What am I gonna do? How do I get the boys to Irving by 5:30 again with bad traffic? I had to think real fast. I went back to my job afterwards, went down every register

"Hey can you switch days with me?"

No sorry I already have plans"

"It's okay"

I would then turn to the next person, "Hey can you switch days with me? I know its short notice but . . ."

"No, if you would have told me earlier maybe I could have."

I kept going, by now I want to cry. "Hey is there any way you can switch days with me tomorrow?"

I wasn't through saying tomorrow when he said, "Sure."

It's a dream come true, I didn't want to work with that b!@#% anyway. I exclaimed, "Okay thanks, see you Thursday bye!"

It gets real busy right before the yearly boxing tournament. I survived it. (Thank you God) When I went to bed at night seemed like I slept 3 hours and back at it again. I exhausted myself. That's how it was for the next couple of years. If I would have had a boyfriend, I think he would have left me or he would have been the one taking the kids to Irving and Grand Prairie.

It's always been said, he will not give you more than you can handle. I got pretty close; I don't know it was tough. At the end, things worked out. It was always at the end, he still made it happen. You can't have pity for yourself. There's just no time for that. In my mind, being so busy is how I also made it worse for myself. Not resting, on the go all the time. When they were out for the summer, it seemed like 3 weeks. Then they were playing football. I was trying to make their games. Picking them up from their locker room parking lot. Getting them something to eat on the way home. By the way, at this point no one is speaking to each other. We just want to get home. It was really tough trying to balance all of that. Not only that, because of my arthritis, I was cold on warm days. So I would wear something warm. Tommy would look at me and say "Please tell me you're not wearing that"

I said, "Yes, I am"

Tommy pleaded, "Mom please don't wear that!"

I didn't realize it at the moment, but I was going to be the only one dressed for winter, when everyone else had spring fever. One day he told me "Mom it's gonna be hot tomorrow, so don't do like yesterday and wear blue sweats, an orange long sleeve shirt and black gloves and a green hat"

Ouch! I said, "Oh sh*t Tommy did I really wear that?"

He replied, "Yeah. I can even bring you the clothes you wore; it's over there by the trash can. You and James just don't care about what clothes you put on in the morning. James is just as colorful as you are."

So much has happened. They were both in the tournament in 2008 and they both won. I always told them if one wins and one loses remember it's okay, we're here to support each other. I warned them not to be mad at each other. No matter the outcome. Tommy had a teacher in elementary he really looked up to. Mr. T, that teacher went to the boxing tournament to support Tommy. I will never forget that. His elementary P.E. teacher Mrs. D. B, always talks to him when she sees him.

She has always been good to Tommy and Tommy always talks about her and says he will never forget her even if she had to get on to him. In Middle school it was his math teacher Mr. C. Tommy really didn't like his teachers but when he did, he really did. I always taught him to respect his teachers, once there it wasn't always like that but I did teach both of my kids to respect their elders, the handicap and how to be courteous to girls. If they did or didn't in school I don't know, but I did teach them.

Vacation

I told my boy's when we were living at my mom's house. Not "if" I ever got back on my feet but "when" I got back on my feet, I will take you each on a cruise for your 10th birthday. Oh their 10th birthday came so fast and I kept my promise. I took them to Cozumel, Mexico. Tommy in 2006 and James in 2008. Of course they both went on each one's trip. I would never take one and leave the other. They loved it, but Tommy got sea sick and said he would never go again. Now he is older and wants to go to Jamaica, because I went and now he seen pictures and wants to go. He says he is ready to get on a ship again. He really deserves it, both of them do.

I have been to Montego Bay Jamaica twice, it was beautiful. A couple of my friends at work and even a manager jokingly call me Stella. We loved it, so this will be cruise #3 for them and cruise #5 for me. I have to squeeze in vacation because if I don't it will not happen. That's what I mean; if you really want something you have to work at it. I never even imagined going on one cruise, much less 4. I just make payments throughout the year. All year long I'm slowly buying what

I need. I'm not a last minute person. I buy clothes, jewelry, shoes and I'm ready to go at the end of the year.

Our first cruise was special. Don't think I wasn't scared, I was. My friend and I decided we would rent a car and go. The week we were leaving my mom calls me, says that my sister told her she would go drop us off and pick us up. So don't worry about renting a car.

I heard through the grapevine {laughing} that my sister had told my mom "Houston traffic is tough, I really don't see Irene doing it. I'm worried, I rather take them myself".

I was so glad, who cares what she thinks. It was packed with cars and raining when we passed Houston. She never said give me gas money or anything. She must have been real worried about my driving. She is a driver, if there was a road to China she would go. I'm a driver because I have to, but long distance I like to relax and not drive. That's exactly what I did. Thanks for the ride.

Groceries

I hate throwing food away and there was a time when I found myself doing that a lot. We would come home to sleep and shower and be gone again early the next day. So our groceries would expire. Going to the store after work to get groceries was not fun. I was tired, my legs hurt and the boys would always say, "We don't like that."

I would tell them to make a sandwich.

"I don't like bread."

I came up with a solution. Not a good one, but it worked. When I was so tired and hurting I would go to the grocery store, told the boys to grab a basket and go their separate ways.

They each got their own groceries and they would call me from inside the store to let me know they were finished, and I would go in and just pay. I killed two birds with one stone. They liked the groceries, because they bought them and two, I didn't have to walk around the grocery store. My grocery bill was higher but we weren't wasting food. I would not have bought half of the things they bought.

I do not like glow in the dark fruit snacks or anything to drink that is blue green.

If I had to take them to buy other things they needed like at the mall, I'm not a mall person but my kids are and I only take them if they need to buy something. We never go just to walk around are you kidding me? My boys would be so impatient with me (James). When I was so tired and hurting, I would take them to buy what they needed. In this case James had such a big heart and was very sweet to tell me, "Mom, I don't want to spend the money you saved."

Tommy grabbed all he could and extras. If James spent $75.00 Tommy would spend $175.00 when he wanted something he did whatever he could to get it. James would always tell me, "It's okay, I will wait till next time".

It was cold and cloudy one day and yes I was hurting so bad. I had told Tommy I would buy him some new tennis shoes. We got some dinner after work and by the end of the day I was no good to go to the mall. Tommy was driving and I hinted two or three times that the mall would be too much for me. Believe it or not it didn't matter to Tommy. He drove to the mall and said, "I will drop you off at the door and I will go park."

I can barely get out of the car, James comes around to help me, he looks at Tommy and say's in a loud voice. "Can this not wait till another day Tommy?"

"No just go in and sit down, the lady already knows me, so I will just take mom's debit card and I.D. and we will be in and out in no time."

He got his shoes; I don't recommend always letting this happen. That day had been set for him so that's why I let it happen and I wasn't going all the way in. Other than that yes, I have put off buying things for Tommy. He deserves a lot, but he has to realize that things sometimes have to be put off. It was hard for him to hear that at first but he has it down now.

Growing up to fast

I always have wondered why Tommy has always wanted to be an adult, or just older than he is. When he was 5 he wanted to be 10. When he was 10 he wanted to be a teenager, now he is 15 and wants to be 25. I really don't know why. He had been looking for a job, without my permission. I said, "Who said you can be employed at 15."

So he replied, "I just want to work to help you pay the bills."

I did feel bad after he told me that. I said, "No, it's okay Tommy I got this." The next day I call him from work.

"Hey Tommy, what are you doing?"

"Sorry gotta go mom, I have 2 haircuts lined up for today".

"Tommy you don't cut hair"

"I do now."

I thought oh sh*t, poor kids.

Before I could say anything he answered, "Ivan let me use his dads clippers"

"Alright, good luck! Warn those kids that I do not want to meet their parents over this. Better not screw up Tommy."

I soon bought him his own clippers. He started lining boys up and did haircuts on the porch. He graduated to the back room where there is a dresser and mirror, and a radio. There were days when I would relax in bed and James comes in tears.

"Mom, look what Tommy did to my hair"

"Why did you let him? I warned you"

"Mom, Tommy is gonna try to fix my hair".

James said he feels bad for Tommy and that's why he lets him, but a couple weeks later.

James angrily says, "Mom look what Tommy did!"

"Go on, get out of here, I don't want to hear it."

"He keeps using me."

And so I tell him, "No, you keep letting him"

Now months have passed and Tommy is doing much better, thanks to James's head. He tells me, that it's in his heart to become a barber. My arthritis still hurts, not near as much, but I told him I would do whatever it took to get him through barber school. If I have to drag myself to work, I will put him through barber school. I know God will help me through this, just like he has helped me with everything else.

Work

I t is now 2012, almost 10 years at that job. Things are becoming a little more difficult for me. I'm 45 years old and arthritis has taken a toll on my body. People help me all the time. I love the customers; I know so many of them by name, and they have become part of my life. I think about leaving and I get emotional. I know this is my heaven sent job, and I wasn't just going to give it up so easy. Not because someone made me mad or even because I was hurting. Sometimes I ask myself if God is testing me. I have been in pain, but I'm not hearing voices telling me that I can't do my job anymore, but I do pick up on red flags. I love cashiering, but there has been so many changes and other things added to cashiering that has made it totally different to what I was used to. No, not everything stays the same all the time, but getting use to this has taken a while for me.

If I didn't let pain get in my way I'm surly not gonna let a few new rules do it. I have made some mistakes there. Mistakes people made and lost their jobs over.

We were very busy one day, and there were these two ladies that came through my line. I helped them, I scanned all their things. I finished the transaction and as far as I know, they leave. A few minutes later I glanced over to the café and I saw them having lunch. I turned around and started helping the person that was next.

As I continued to work, that same lady walks up to me and taps me on the shoulder and says, "Excuse me, Ma'am, you gave me too much money." Then she handed me $93.00. "mija, you were only supposed to give me .93 cents back."

To tell you the truth, I don't even know if I thanked her. All I remember is my heart dropping. My poor heart was dropped so many times. That has happened to me like 4 or 5 times. No lie!

I would wait for weeks to go by before I told anyone, like that it would be old news. What are the chances of people always giving you the money back? Some do, some don't. I just believe God was taking care of me.

One day I was talking to my friend about one of those past transactions. She couldn't believe it. She kept saying, "Are you serious?"

Well, later that day, I had one happen to me, right in front of her face. A couple was in line and was ready to pay. The bill totaled $275.00 and some change. He said he was going to pay $200 cash and the rest on a check for $75. He gave me the $200.00 but wasn't sure if he had counted the $200.00 correctly. I counted the money and it was correct, so I entered $275.00 cash. He kept insisting on giving me a check for $75.00 and some change. I kept saying no! My supervisor was right next to him which means she was standing right in front of me, giving me the evil eye. He went on for a few minutes about still owing me $75.00 dollars.

Finally, the lady who was next said, "Irene, take the check. Your money is gonna come up short. He is being honest with you."

Then, I woke up. I finally realized he was right. My point is, he gave me the money. After it was all over with, I asked my supervisor, "Why didn't you say anything, you saw it all?"

She answered, "I just froze because we had just talked about those things happening to you."

Another time three of us in one week were short of money. I got so nervous when my manager told me, but she was real nice about it. I remember I was going downstairs and she was going up when she told me. They did all of their investigating and from all 3 of us there was no money to be found anywhere.

A couple of days past, I lost the money first then they did, but we all did it in the same week. Later that week I was counting my money in our counting room where we have calculators and money bags and a place to turn it in. One of the girls that lost money that week walked into the room crying. I asked her what was wrong. She said, "Oh I just got written up for the money but they were so rude to me."

Then the next day I saw the second girl. She wasn't saying much at first, and then she just said, "I better not get one more slip or I'm out".

I asked, "Did you get one today?"

She said, "Yes, I just got it right before I came up here."

I didn't say anything else I just continued to count my money. I just wanted to clock out and go. It's been 4 years now since all this happened and no one called me into the office. Only when my manager asked me about it and that was it. Safe again! Who is taking care of me? God. I did sign a slip, but my shift supervisor gave it to me, and I signed it on my own time and just handed it back to her. No one took me to the office. That didn't mean I wasn't worried about it, I was.

I thank God every day for a lot of things. When I'm leaving my driveway, I asked him to run my register and to help me give the correct money back. I ask him to give me the strength that I need to last 8 hours. I talk to God like he is sitting in the passenger seat. After I'm through praying and talking, I feel like I know he heard me. I know I'm going to have a good day. I feel safe after I pray.

There were days when my leg hut so bad at work that when I went to lunch I just wanted to elevate it. One day I was starving but I was not going to go upstairs, clock out and then go back down stairs. This guy was on his cell phone saying, "It's okay babe just stay right there, I'm on my way."

He turns and says, "Here eat this sub, I gotta go my wife broke down." A sub, chips and drink, what are the chances?! Right before I bit into that delicious sandwich I just said thank you God for this lunch. I could go on and on.

Like the time my car drove very smoothly until I got to my parking spot then it overheated badly. Then another time, again a smooth ride but when I turned into my driveway it sounded like a huge set of drums fell on the concrete, I said, "Lord."

What in the world is going on with this car. It got me home first, and then broke down. Thank you God.

Tommy's Happiness

When I went to bed at night, pain hit hard. It's always worse at night time, it's like my body finally started to relax, then the pain would attack, all I wanted was silence. I wanted to rest, Tommy would be in the next room watching R&B. It was all about professional skateboarding. The skateboarding sound bothered me real bad. Then there was that girls laughed too. For weeks after we got cable I couldn't understand why he would watch that almost every night and it seemed like every night there was a small argument.

I would yell, "Tommy turn it down!"

He simply replied, "Okay."

It seemed to me like it was the same thing over and over daily. I love reading, and one night I was reading a book and both boys were in their room. They were watching R&B again.

I shouted, "Close that door or turn it down, I'm trying to relax a little".

Tommy answered, "Yes ma'am."

Then again, they were both laughing so loud. I was getting really mad. Then, I stopped to think for a moment, at the same time I thought, behind all that skateboarding is a beautiful sound; my boys laughing. I got up and went to the room and they immediately turned it down.

I said "No turn it back up its okay." I know they both wanted to faint, but I thought to myself why not? It's their room, their TV. I got cable for them, now I want silence. It's not fair, I went back to my room and just listened to them laugh. If I'm always in pain then when do they have a chance to laugh? On my days off they would want to do whatever they could for me before they left.

Tommy says, "Here is a big glass of water for you in case you can't get up. The TV is ready and it's on the channel you like."

"Thank you son, have a good day at school. I love you."

A few weeks later he says again, "You need anything, we're leaving."

"No, I'm okay. Thank you son."

Saying I love you is an everyday thing for us. Not one day goes by that I don't tell my kids I love them and they tell me too.

"We're leaving mom, love you. TV is ready, the remote is on the bed."

When they leave I go back to sleep and wake up a couple hours later. I go get the remote to watch TV and it's programmed to "R&B." Oh no! This can't be. I push every button and I find myself watching R&B. I had no choice, so I was like okay, this episode is not too bad. It's finally over and another one starts. So I just quit trying. I didn't change the channel anymore. I just sat there and watched it. I couldn't believe it but I was enjoying it. It was a pretty good episode. It was where a rock band shows up in a big truck and then they all end up rocking out with them. When my boy's got home I told them what happened and they couldn't believe it. Tommy started apologizing.

I said, "It's okay guys I actually enjoyed it."

After that happened Tommy would say :

Tommy: "Mom, you sleeping?"

Mom: "No, just reading."

Tommy: "Come over here with us, watch this show you will like it."

Mom: "Okay guys, be right there."

Mom: "Oh my gosh ! Guy's this is crazy, what is this?"

Tommy: "It's called Ridiculous Things".

Oh no! More R&B, needless to say I watch them both now.

About James

My son James is the youngest. James tells me, he now feels like he didn't help enough. Crazy, if you ask me. James is younger; he wanted to do kid things. He had a lot of little cars, and I mean a lot.

Tommy did help a lot more but it was because Tommy was feeling my pain. Tommy's mind is ahead of him anyway.

I told James if I was sick you would play with your cars. Rolling them and making the driving sound, entertaining himself. He loved coloring and drawing, so all of that helped me. Plus he did help me by saying silly things that cheered me up. Something I took to heart was when he was playing, coloring, or whatever it was, and he decided he was done. He dropped what he was doing and go cuddle up to me, hug me, or give me like 2 big kisses and he was out. He never went to his bed first. He was always where I was, but he did help a lot more than he actually remembers. Now, he is tough on me. He gets mad because he says Tommy babies me, he doesn't.

James is firm with me. If we go to a restaurant he moves the salt out of the way. It's okay because I know what it can cause but I do love salt. If we are walking and he is holding my hand he will say, "A little bit faster mom," or "Don't look down at your feet, just walk".

When he knows I do want some salt on my food he puts a little on his hand then sprinkles it on. Home therapy has made me cry in the past, but it's gotten a lot better. He tells me, "If it hurts a little keep going" or "Try not to cry, because you still have 15 more minutes left." I think it's good because it has helped that he is a little tough on me.

One thing I love about him is when he sees me from far away he opens his arms like to give me a big hug, that's when I know he has been missing me. This happens when our schedules are totally different; I work and he is home or he has school projects and is out working on them and I'm at home. I go to bed to rest for the next day, and he gets home late. So now he is asleep and I get up and leave early. So now it's only a kiss on the forehead for whoever is the one sleeping.

We look forward to Sundays. On Sundays we know were going to be together. Summer time we like to go out to eat. Winter time I love to cook a big Sunday meal. When I'm cooking, James will be organizing his room right next to the kitchen, he will be showing me things he has been saving and telling me about his week. What he did, and what happened in school and just catch up on things.

He can also be a little sneaky, especially when it comes to driving. He can only do it, if I don't feel good and I must be with him. Not too long ago I was cooking a Sunday dinner and I made a big pitcher of lemon flavored tea, a drink that James and I both like, and I put it in the fridge. I was getting plates ready and just walking in the kitchen when he all of a sudden walks in with a big fountain drink and some chips.

"Hi mom, food almost ready?" But never looked at me. I kept staring at him and he knew I was looking at him. He wanted to laugh I could tell.

I was serious, I said, "James you sure did walk to the store fast, you were just in your room."

No answer.

"Look at me James!"

Then the big laugh came out. "Mom I need a little snack before I eat."

I just kept staring at him.

Then he finally tells me, "Sorry, but I didn't walk. I took your car, but I just went to the one that's real close. Sorry, really!"

I'm serious. My keys stay in my pocket or somewhere in the house that I'm certainly not going to mention. I went to an arts and crafts show and bought a cute keys board that is now a decoration. Nope, my keys do not hang there anymore. That's trouble just waiting to happen.

James is a lot calmer than Tommy. When I'm at work, he will leave me a text. "I'm home, order a pizza please." He use to walk to go get a pizza, but it's a little far, and he is not embarrassed to be walking home with a box of pizza. So now I order it, and pay with my credit card and I have it delivered. If he has a good movie, pizza, games, and drinks in the refrigerator he is a happy kid. Doesn't take much to make him happy, especially if he knows I'm on my way home. Now we're both happy.

A Priceless Moment

I was at home one day, the boys found a bike with no front tire and they wanted me to fix it up. Of course I said "No".

Months went by and that bike stayed in the back yard. So one day I was cooking I said, "Tommy, ya'll come inside dinner is ready."

Tommy answers, "Wait I'm next to go for my ride, James is coming down the hill."

I ask, "On what?"

"Our bike," Tommy said.

"Ya'll don't have a bike," I say.

"Yes we do," reassures me, "look James is coming."

I froze. I stepped on to the front porch and there comes James. They got that broken bike, got a dark green grocery cart, propped the front part of the bike on to the bottom of the cart, tied wire on it so that it would not come loose. So the handle to the grocery cart now became the handle bars and the 4 wheels on the cart became the front tire. I could not believe my eyes, I loved it so much. It didn't stop there;

on the side of the cart they tied a big sign that I had that said the name of our basketball team. I'm telling you that has been one of my favorite things that they have done.

Yes, he was right. He proved to me that they had a bike. We had it for about 2 weeks. Then one day this truck pulls up with about 10 more carts just like that one. They were picking up carts that people take home so we had to give it up. It made me a little sad. Oh well, it's okay. The boys were young so they were very disappointed too. They went out to the porch and told that guy, "If you want it, you're going to have to take it apart" and that guy did. Took him like 45 minutes to undo all the wire, but he took the cart.

Old Fashioned Rules

I know I get on my kids nerves. They are getting older and my old fashioned rules still stand. Old fashioned has helped me. I wasn't a very young mom and trust me, they let me know. They say I went too far for not letting them have anything with wheels, which I don't regret because I heard of a lot of accidents.

If I wasn't around to watch them then they couldn't be alone and riding a bike. Seems selfish but at least they have all their teeth and their in one piece. James skateboards a little now but growing up they did not have bikes or skateboards or owned roller blades. The closest Tommy came to wheels was when the tennis shoes came out with folding wheels on the bottom. James had a scooter but not for long. They had big plastic hot wheel cycles when they were younger and yes they did own tricycles but those times were not dangerous for me. I know they rode their friend's bikes when I wasn't around and borrowed stuff when I was at work.

Actually one day I went to pick up Tommy at the baby sitters, they were outside. He saw me so he got on a ramp with the bike and fell, landed right on his mouth. I almost wrecked into the sitters nice truck. He never cried, I was thinking the worse. He did chip his front tooth. He also had a fat lip for a couple of days. See there, what did I tell you . . .

Easter Sunday 2012

I had the worst Easter ever. I had not been that sick in about 2 years but that day I did not get out of bed. We had plans but did not make them, I mean how could I? And the boys were back to waiting on me. "What can I do Mom?" or "what do you want to watch?"

I felt so bad, they were already dressed. Their cousin called and invited them to their Easter cook out. I heard Tommy say, "No, thanks my mom doesn't feel good but thanks anyways."

"Who was that?" I asked.

He explained to me what he said and I said, "Please, go."

But Tommy said, "No we don't want to leave you alone."

I said, "If you go I will feel better, the park is close to the house and I want you all to go somewhere for Easter."

"Are you sure?" Tommy asked

I tell him, "Yes, please go. I will be sleeping anyway"

They went and they kept calling and checking on me. When they got back first thing James did was check my water to see if it was room temperature. He said let me get you some more ice water. Tommy started checking to see if my knee brace was loose. What a blessing God gave me.

The Following Sunday

The Sunday after Easter, No surprise I was hurting. I was resting in my room. I had let the boy's go to their friends house. Tommy wanted a new hat. I had got him some money from the ATM the day before. When I was asleep he woke me up. He had a couple of friends with him.

Tommy: "You will never believe what I did!"

I don't know why but I said "Tommy, don't play with me. What did you do?"

Tommy: "I got a big tattoo on my back, it's really big!"

I believed him. He has always loved tattoos. When he was little he would put stickers all over his arms and chest.

"Mom, are you ready to look?" Before I could react he picked up his shirt and nothing. I was so relieved. However, ten seconds later he showed me a REAL one on his chest over his heart. It was my name with a beautiful rose.

I was supposed to surprise him and take him. I knew that he wanted my name on his chest but not now. He was too young for a tattoo, and I cried because I know that tattoos are there for life.

He was hugging me, saying "You know how proud I am to be wearing your name on my heart?"

I knew he was proud of that, but I still wish he would have waited at least four more years. But he was hugging me, because he was guilty of it. I really wanted to know who had made the tattoo but he never told me. I think it's best that it stays that way. I was very disappointed in him, and it took me about two months to get over it. I did tell him to never forget that my dying wish is for them not to ever get one on their neck or hands. That's just me, but at least he didn't get dots on his knuckles. Now that I would have scrubbed off myself. He did promise me he would never get another one . . . . until he's of age.

James claims that he really isn't into tattoos, but that is sure to change. And trust me I'm in no hurry for that.

My Job

I have been at my job almost ten years now, but things seem to be getting more difficult for me now. I'm 45 years old now and arthritis has taken a toll on my body.

In a way it's okay because I already survived the worst. Now my body just feels banged up.

My job has been good to me. I mean I still had my bad days and then my really bad days, but for the most part my time at work has been good.

There is stress at work, my stress stems from trying to juggle everything at once. But it wouldn't be called work if it was supposed to be easy. But my co-workers and customers have definitely helped make my job easier. There were times when I was very stressed at work and even thought of quitting on a daily basis. The stress didn't even have anything to do with the pain, but now I can actually put some of the pain aside.

There were days at work that I would just have to look beyond the pain. If I stopped everything just because I hurt, my entire world would come to a stop. Then what? I don't know and I don't want to know because the outcome would not be good.

But there are problems at all jobs. At this age I want to start eliminating problems. I'm not sure how far this job will take me, it's just up for me to decide. I don't know where I'm going, but I tell you, I sure know where I've been. All you single moms and dads find a way to make things better for your kids. No one is going to provide for them like you can. Work your hardest, and give it all you've got.

I'm still a cashier and my job is once again going smooth. My kids have basically grown up there. I took them to almost all my work meetings, and almost all my work meetings were at 9:00 at night. I would go home do what I had to do. I never wanted to ask anyone to watch them because they already been in school all day and went to the afterschool program for a few hours. So I just asked if I could bring my kids to the meeting because I had no other choice. So I did.

The boys honestly didn't like it because we were all tired, but it was just part of my job. They would fall asleep on me, and they fit perfectly on the café tables. So I would lay them down on those seats, it wasn't the softest place for them but it worked. Then people from the meeting would help me carry one of them to the car.

So please, do whatever you have to do. I did. Make phone calls, ask questions. Jobs can be tough to handle but just never give up.

I thank God for my job, especially for the elevator we have. Yes, I thought about quitting in stressful times but I know I'm stronger than that. I just go home, rest and think about what happened, and how I can fix it and go back the next day. I just work at it. That's what we all have to do. Just pray it can be resolved.

Cashiers

ashiers at my job have come and gone. I try to get along with everyone and I think I do a pretty good job of that. Most of it comes naturally and many of the cashiers really do like me. They help me as much as they can. If they don't have any customers at their register, they come to mine.

We have a register, where big orders come through. We all have to work that lane at least a couple of hours out of our shift. It's a lot of work, but I'm used to it. I'm also the oldest cashier there. There used to be an older lady than me but she quit, making me the oldest. After a couple years she came back, so now she is the oldest again (laughing). I think we're taking turns being the oldest.

The other cashiers both male and female show a lot of respect for me. My friends Ashton and John Medina would always say, "Call me if you have a big order, we'll move it for you."

When I first started there I worked that heavy lane all day long, for at least a couple of years until rules changed. So that's why I'm used to it, but I'm older now and even more body parts hurt. But I'm lucky to have people who really show concern. That helps the soul also. Things are better at work now, I'm not too stressed and that makes my boys happy too. The new cashiers think I'm hurting really bad, but the worst has already passed. But I do still thank everyone daily for their concern.

Here at work we all help each other, so, when I'm not busy I go and help another cashier at their register but they never let me lift the heavy stuff. I just try to help as much as I can so I can be fair. Even a tiny girl that was about to have a baby was telling me, "Oh, when that lady with all the drinks is ready to be rung up call me so I can help you." Of course I didn't call her; there was no possible way I would ever let that happen. When I work the lane near the café, the ladies always keep an eye on me, they either take people from my line or literally come and do my job for me. I really thank God daily for their help.

No time for anything

I missed a lot when my kids were growing up. But I know that as a single mother if I wanted to provide for my kids, then I had to work. I tried to do and see as much as I could. I missed my kids even though we lived together. Seems like my days off are so busy and they go by so fast. They would make plans to go somewhere with their friends and their parents on weekends which ruled me out. But I was at work every weekend. My job sometimes had me working crazy hours, I'm at work all the time. Yes, thank god for a job, but it is still tough on you when your trying to balance your job, your kids, sports, a house, everything that comes with the house, and most important, my health, because ready or not here it comes. I work 9:30 am to 6 pm or 11 to 7. I'm there morning, noon, afternoon, and going into the evening. Leaving no time for anything I come home, we eat dinner, and then I'm in bed. The boys stay up do a little homework or watch a movie, and go to bed. They leave to school and I'm sleeping. I get up get ready for work, now I work 12 noon to close, which means I'm out of there after 9:30 pm. I come home and the boys are asleep (not always) but most of the time that means they get their own dinner and did their own thing. Now bed time which means I saw them a little bit in the morning and that's it. I feel like I'm wasting precious time and I think, is it always going to be like this, even when they're older? Even though they are teenagers they know we're not always together and they also want more time with me. If they have in service days at school for teachers they ask, "Do you really have to go to work today ?." I leave the house in plenty of time to get to work but I always rush home. If they have to go somewhere it's like "mom hurry, I told them I would be there as soon as possible" or "hurry I can't be late to practice." It's always rush, rush, rush. For what? It just means more time apart. While they were gone I would do a little grocery shopping, I would be in line to pay and I would get a phone call, "Mom come get me, they canceled for today, hurry it's hot-out here. I'm running crazy daily. I told my friends at work something has got to give. I don't know what but something really does have to give. My job and my kids keep me very busy. I have given both of them everything I have, I gave them my all, and they sure took all I had.

When I started writing this book, I didn't tell anyone, but one close friend and of course the boys. That was just in case something went wrong. So I kept it to myself. I told people I was working on a project and asked for prayers over it. I was at work one day, and now cashiering had become tremendously stressful. I left my register pouring down sweat and went to my friend Ashton and said, "Today is the day. I want them to fire me, I'm ready, I just don't care anymore."

After I said that and walked back to my register it was a great deal of relief. It seemed like it took twenty pounds of pressure off my shoulders. Here I am, a single mother of two paying bills, rent, and everything else and saying "I don't care anymore," really says a lot. Ashton just looked at me, kind of surprised that I said that. What I loved lately was the end of my shift, knowing I was going home to write. I would just continue where I left off. Like I said, time just flew by when I was writing. If I started writing after work at 8:30 or nine at night, it would seem to me like it had been two hours but it was already 3 in the morning. Sometimes I think getting fired would have been a big relief. But deep down I didn't want that, My body feels banged up. Things seemed to be falling into place, but it's happening outside my job. The people knew I didn't feel good, they asked me all the time if I was okay.

My kids would say, "Mom, I wish it were all men who shopped there, so they can help you."

I looked at them and said, "You will be surprised at all the women who help me! They move almost everything for me."

"Really mom?" Tommy let out a sigh of relief, "That makes me happy."

I don't want to miss any more of my children's childhood. When it was cold and rainy and my son James had football practice in the morning. I was sick, stiff and hurting from that weather. He walks up to my bed about 6:30 am. "Mom, I'm almost ready okay?" I didn't know how to tell him I couldn't get up. I closed my eyes again and just prayed.

I told him, "James, baby I'm hurting so bad, just take the car, it's early and no children are out right now."

"Really mom," His eyes got as big as a 50 cent coin. "I can take the car?!"

I told him what streets to take and where to park. It was always a big relief when he walked back in at 7:45. But I know all of this was taking a big risk. When it was too cold or when it was raining, I just prayed every time. The power of prayer is unbelievably powerful. I love it.

Wanting me time

I would love more time for me. *Me time*. Sounds so good and relaxing. I would like to do yoga, but there is no time for it. I tried it once at a work out place. The other ladies were excellent and all had wonderful balance, but me. The instructors told us to put both hands on the floor in front of us. I did do that but when it came to picking up one leg slowly, I fell to the side. I have no balance and I laughed like a crazy lady. I need more yoga time.

I hardly get the chance to do my nails or my hair. I would also love to drop off and pick up the boys from school more. My sweet little James would love that. I would love to have a therapist, more than anything, that's what I need. But where do I find the time? I have to change something. Retail is never going to change. I'm going to do whatever I can and leave the rest to God! I would love to volunteer at a food bank, but no time. Relax in the middle of the day with a good book or movie. This doesn't have to seem impossible. It can happen. Now, I am better than I was health wise, I don't hurt at night like I used to. Mornings are also easier. Good gosh, nowhere near the way It used to be. I have learned a lot about arthritis through the years. The eating, stretching, and walking, my boys do a lot of therapy with me. They told me, please don't say that we used to say arthur-ritis. But I just laughed. It's part of it, and that's how it was. I loved to hear them say that, it cheered me up.

Church

We go to church as much as we can. It's an all-black church, Greater Worth Hill Missionary Baptist Church. It's a great church. I have gone as a visitor to several churches with friends that invite me from work. One day after going to have lunch with my friend, we stopped by her moms house. My friend introduced me to her mom, we quickly became good friends. After a few months she also invited me to their church. I went with my kids a couple of times. Then one day the church had a 25 year celebration and she invited me as her special guest. I will never forget that. She also had a downfall (cancer) after she was not here anymore I continued to go to the church. The boys love her husband. The boys also love going there. Tommy went bowling with the youth group, and he had a great time. I love it when I know my kids are having a good time. People there are very very friendly. When we first went they treated us like they had known us for a long time. I love the singing and we find peace there.

I was raised a Catholic and I baptized my boys in a Catholic Church. The ladies who sing in the church choir at Greater Worth Hill sing beautiful. A couple of ladies have invited me to sing with them a couple of times. No way. I said no. They must want the people to take off running. I personally would love to, but I wouldn't dare, "I CAN'T SING!" My friend sang she was just the loveliest lady ever. She was our Mama Wade. That's what we called her. The preaching is beautiful. Sometimes I turn to tell Tommy something and he is teared up. I just turn away. I want to ask him, but whatever the reason I just leave it alone. My mom says as long as your serving God, it doesn't matter where you go. I don't look at religion. She is right, we're serving God. I'm teaching my kids how important church is, and how important it is to pay your church tithes. People at church have come up to me to tell me that they can tell how much the boys love me, just by looking at how they act with me.

My Parents

My parents were so much help to me. I moved out when I was thirty years old. I know, shame on me. But it wasn't like they had been trying to get rid of me. I was always working and we got along very well. After I moved out Tommy was born. I didn't have the baby blues, I had the parent blues. I wanted to go back so bad. But then that passed. When I started having problems in my relationships, I couldn't just ignore it and go to another room, it meant grabbing the kids and go. Just go. If they didn't have on shoes or a jacket, didn't matter, my parents lived close by. I would stay one or two days out of the weekend. It happened several times. But every time after the weekend was almost over I would go back to my house. Hoping things would be better. But they weren't. When I was there, I remember my mom would just listen so patiently to my problems. Then she would give me her advice. She was so good to me. That's why I didn't want to ask to stay there after it was official that I would never be back with him. I didn't stay there until months later. I didn't want them to know just yet that things had really gotten out of control, but everybody knew. It was no secret. But once I started staying there again, both my mom and dad were very good to me and the boys. I talked to my mom more about my personal issues than my dad, He is very laid back. He knew something was wrong but didn't ask much at all. To him as long as me and the boys were physically okay, then he wasn't going to do much talking.

My mom was there for me like no one has ever been. When I was talking to her she would be moving my hair back out of my face or just listening and had her arm around me. I'm so glad I have them, I love them so much. That is a true blessing. I know I have said so many times that I was in pain but the time I got really really sick I stayed with them a couple of days. I slept with her and I didn't want her to see me in so much pain, so I held back the tears. But I went to sleep and she woke me up. Just the motherly love in her she put her hand right on the pain and she asked *"Donde te duele?"* ("Where does it hurt?")

She gave me my medicine and just knowing I was there and she was taking care of me made things much better. It was good for my soul. I tried walking the best I could and just made sure she didn't see the worst of it, because she is my mother and I would not want to see my child in so much pain.

My mom is a strong woman. She is strong in many ways. To her it doesn't matter what age you are she is there for her children, both her and my dad. My dad has taken me to work so many times and I just enjoy his company when we're in the car. Every time he sees me he will ask how I feel. Or if I talk to him on the phone that's the first thing he asks, "How's your leg today?"

I visit them any chance I get. I have breakfast with my mom a lot and my dad he loves banana splits. I enjoy going to get one and taking it to him. And of course, he loves to see me drive up. I thank God every day for them.

The Boys now 13 and 15

My boys are getting older now. It's been a very long road. It's a bit different now, but for the most part a good road. James is still a big kid at heart. Tommy can be, but he prefers older. James is also real into his school work, Tommy is not. James likes to make homemade sling shots and play video games with his friends. Tommy is cutting hair and lifting weights. I can still trust James to do and go just about anywhere. They pretty much still follow my rules; I just have a problem with Tommy wanting more freedom. That's crazy if you ask me. He has too much is my problem. I give them time to visit with friends, but it's just never enough for them. They still help me; they are still very good to me, especially Tommy. Tommy is 50/50 he can be a real good kid but then he can turn around and do bad. Tommy is unpredictable; he is the one that has poured his heart out to me. He has cried with me and for me, he has been my little doctor.

Sadly he has also been the one to give me the most problems. I can still say nothing major. He doesn't fight in school, he doesn't fight on the streets, and he doesn't rob people or houses. None of that stuff thank the good lord! My boy's know very well that I have laid down the law on them. Do this, don't do that. They are like day and night, completely different. The way they look, act and dress. One light complected, one dark, one tall, one short, a big appetite and a small appetite. Even at birth one in the winter and one in the summer. Tommy was born early in the morning and James close to midnight. They have a lot of time on their hands to do bad things if they wanted. I'm lucky that they do think about some of the things I tell them. They know to be home by the time I get home. I hate having to look for them after work. Tommy likes to talk back and tries to raise his voice. Yes my hands hurt but they both know, that if they think they're going to yell at me, I don't have a problem swinging.

My hand may hurt a little but I'll be fine. When I don't let Tommy go somewhere that starts an argument. He can have a little temper, and he will push my buttons to see what all he can get away with. He wants to walk to his friend's house at 9:30 or 10:00 at night. Heck no! There is a curfew. Every one follows it but Tommy. He is not out that late but if it was up to him he would walk at midnight. If I'm in for the night so are they. I can't sleep if my boys are not home. They do have 3 male role models in their life and have been for a long time. James will start high school in august and Tommy; this was his first year in High school. It has gone by fast. I want to get better, so that I can help them further their education. I want to see some college in their future. James wants to go to college. Tommy wants to go to barber school. I really want to be there for the boys just like they were there for me. I had always thought Tommy being 13,14 and now 15, it hasn't been too bad, I was actually proud of myself. I told my mom I don't know what the rest of my kids teenage years are going to be like, but if I have problems I will just have to face them like all parents before me have. James is very laid back. He is like a calm country boy, Tommy is wall street. He makes plans without asking me, and thinks it's okay. A lot of people had warned me about teenage years, especially my older sister.

I thought to myself, well I believe I have done good with Tommy so far. There were some difficult days but I thought I still have things under control.

A couple more years and I should be okay. No problem. "GOOD GOSH ALMIGHTY" 15 ½ took a turn. I'm like "what" now more than ever he wants to be out. Boy, me and Tommy bump heads now. He wants to explain to me why he is right, and why it should be his way. It's a one side argument with him. I tell him, hell no! He throws in that he helped me, well yeah, you did, but I done told both of them. You helping me doesn't mean you run my life now. No way, but good try. When he is on the phone at night I hear him telling his friend;

Tommy: "Aye foo, I'll be right over" so then I fly up out of bed.
Mom: "Tommy what do you think your doing?"
Tommy: "Nothing Mom, just going to my home boys right quick, told that foo I'm on my way"
Mom: "Call that foo back, tell him you're not going. It's after 10 o'clock. Your crazy as hell."

If I have to stay awake for the next 3 hours I will. I have woke up in the middle of the night to find him gone, my car gone, and he passed a red light and got a ticket in the mail. Then for the next 5 weeks, I slept with him, any move he made I woke up, he hated it. That one did get passed me, but it only made things worse for him after I found out. My friends at work that have already been through the teen age years, they tell me such cool places to hide my keys. I love it. Sometimes when he is mad he says he cant wait to be 18 and leave. Well guess what "Good riddance" because 18 doesn't mean too much to me. It's just the number between 17 and 19. It's not going to prove to me that he is an adult. They both have told me that, I made sure to tell them. Please don't make that famous u-turn and come back. Don't leave mad, and I tell them and tell them and warm them over and over "be ready".

Life out there is not easy, nothing is handed to you. You have to go get it, work for what you need. I don't want my boys to leave mad, that's the last thing I want. When they do become adults and leave, if they leave and they really tried making it on their own but couldn't yes, I'm here! My door will always be open for them. Don't leave with a bully attitude, then return with a bully attitude because that's not for me. I will not support healthy adults. I'm sorry! If it's a friend, a boyfriend, a husband, it doesn't matter. I'm not doing it again. I'm not going to get up, go work and leave a healthy adult sleeping at my house. No way. I go, you go. I have told my kids not to depend on anyone but themselves. I tried covering all the bases on information they should know. Now when they were in pre-school and I knew I was on my own with them, I always told my mom, I will try my best to keep them from hanging with the wrong crowd. Come to find out later people were telling their kids, stay away from Tommy and James. Okay now my kids are the wrong crowd. More so Tommy than James. I would notice some friends would not come around anymore and other mothers would tell me so and so doesn't want their kid around Tommy because he smokes. Oh I'm sorry did you know Tommy smokes. Well I do now. One day Tommy said take me to my friend's house to pick up my CD. I said okay, we all get in the car. When we arrive at his friend's house they are having a little family get together. We didn't get off, the little brother runs to the car and said my mom said James can stay but not Tommy. We busted out laughing, I said we're only getting a CD. Then she came to the car, said hello and for us to get off and join them but it was fake. So we didn't I already knew we were not welcome.

That innocent kid was saying the truth. He was too young to just say that by coincidence. I think it's funny, but if that's how they want to look at it, fine! I'm good, when I see ladies I know at the groceries store. First thing they say, "I saw Tommy walking the other day" I'm like okay. Tommy walks, he's a walker. Everybody sees Tommy walking. Both of my kids have a lot of friends. Most of them live right up the street. Tommy knows a lot of people, and is moody with me (typical) but very friendly to everyone else. James has football practice in the afternoon. So one day Tommy text me I was fixing to get off work. The text said . . . steak? Those are the things I don't want to say no to, because I think about everything they have done for me and they deserve so much more than steak. Well, Tommy has his favorite steak house. I text back, okay be ready. I picked him up. There was very little conversation in the car. At this age, it's normal. I just listen to the radio.

We get there; get a table, we order and we had been talking a little. When we were half way through our meal something about Tommy's behavior got my attention. My motherly instinct, I leaned over the table and I said:

Mom: "Tommy look at me!!" he turned and looked out the window.
Mom: "Look at me right now Tommy"
Tommy: "I'm tired mom, and I'm hungry!"
Mom: "You're high aren't you?"
Tommy: "No"
Mom: "Yes you are, I know tired eyes and I know high eyes and you are high"
Tommy: "Yea, I'm sorry"

I didn't get mad, it saddened me, but as terrible as this may sound I knew this would happen one day. I knew it would be as a teenager. When it actually happened, it got me. It never left my mind, where we were, what we were doing, the time of day, our table. It's all around him. I'm sure no one forced him, he chose to start. I made it real clear to him, since he had done ruined my meal. I said you will never be allowed to come into my house high. Stay where you're at because you're already disrespecting me, now you want to do it right under my nose. You best believe I'll take care of that. It's heart breaking, but I had to remind him, once. Him and James came back from playing basketball. James comes in goes straight to the shower. Tommy comes in right behind him with his cap real low into his face and straight to his room. I went in there tapped him on his cap and said, go back to where you were. When you're not high anymore come back. So he did. Now I tell them go, but when ya'll walk into this door I want you to come straight to me and look me in the eye. I don't know how I'm going to control it for the next couple of years, but he better open his eyes. I will try to do my do my best. That's all I can do, he hates when I find out what he has done that day. He says:

Tommy: "you have people watching me, I know you do" I already know you mom."
Mom: "Good, because I already know you too Tommy."

I have to be firm, speak with everything I got, at the end of the day we all say I love you. Me to them, and them to me. Not brother to brother. I know they love each other. May not show but Tommy loves his brother and will definitely always be there for him. However! They are teenagers and they are my teenagers, and I found out that at this age you are definitely not their friend. That's okay because I don't want to be anyway. I can't back away, I can't back away from bad behavior, instead I have to find a way to work with it and take care of the problem instead of ignoring it. It's been a lot of work. Has it worked for me? Most of it has, Tommy is angry for several personal reasons. I understand him and try to help him as much as I can but Tommy prefers to speak to someone else instead of me and that's okay. He says it's a man thing. Tommy knows older men that have actually done time in the penitentiary.

Those men talk to him and give him the best advice. Not only that, Tommy listens. I really don't know them, but I certainly appreciate them. Both Tommy and James have everything they need and more, but they have one void in their heart. They miss their dad. There's very little contact. Conversations are not too often but when they talk it's just not good. My opinion on teenagers, tough! It has been tough, but talking has done me some good. They are never going to be perfect but as long as they don't use bad language with me and raise their hand to me or really disrespect me I think I'm okay. My main problem right now is smoking and getting Tommy to come home earlier. He is not far at all, but I still worry. If I have to go get him, yes he immediately gets in the car, but by then I'm pissed, I do use bad language. I know when and where and with who. This past summer was a little tough. It's when things started changing with them. I left a few times in the evening, and when I came home there were a few times I would find the cops there. The cop light are such drama, but that's just how it is. Tommy was in a car full of teenagers. That is one thing that I do not allow. The cop told me that the driver did not signal twice, so he pulled them over, right in front of my house. Both my boys were in there and when the police lights went on, they woke up Tommy. I said Tommy that is so embarrassing. He had already been home and was sleepy, but he got up and went anyway. I know I was gone 25 minutes and returned. Before that, Tommy was younger. I went to go get them barbeque sandwiches, gone 15 minutes came home, cops were there. Tommy and his friends went outside to shoot a bb gun. They hit a city truck, the only reason they didn't take them was because the bb's were plastic. Boy's will be boys. If Tommy wants to go somewhere now he says "May I please". I laugh, I love it.

James has done a few himself but not too bad. I know that police officers have to give parents bad news sometimes, but Tommy was really acting up one day. He left, was walking from one friend's house to another friend's. The police saw him and brought him home. He said it too fast, so he never scared me. He knocked, I went to the door, he said "Fort Worth Police we have your son here" it was one in the morning. The police said, he is very respectful, didn't run and is cooperating. So now he is doing community service. He said "Mom this is not fun", I'm sorry, he said, "Mom if I have to work outside can you buy me some dark sunglasses. I'm embarrassed and don't want anyone to recognize me." Hmm! Bad boy Tommy, gotta love em! So in a way I do feel like I have control of them. They know when it comes down to it, It's my voice that counts at the end of the day. I may be shorter than them, but it's me they look up to. Not me to them. Tommy is only 15 but he is learning that I'm not backing down. I'm doing my time with them. Every morning is still a big hug and a kiss from both of them.

We try not to go to bed mad. Especially James, he may not want me to say it but he is still such a mama's boy with me. At home every time he passes by me I say some cariños to him. This means baby talk. He rolls his eyes and laughs. Yes they still help me, both are still there for me. They don't have to help me so much anymore. They tell me all the time that they love and appreciate me for being there for them. That's all I need to hear. Close to the end of the school year I withdrew Tommy from high school. I home schooled him for 2 months. To add to my 5 million other things on my to do list. Tommy just didn't do well in High school. The teachers tried, we had conference after conference. He didn't do terrible things. He just wasn't doing anything at all. No work, if he did he would start it and not finish it and, because it was incomplete he wouldn't turn it in at all, just the same as not doing it at all. He would be the first to fly out of a classroom and then late to his next class. Cutting class he tried that in 8th grade. It was his favorite thing to do.

I put a stop to that. In high school he really couldn't do that. They called me every time he was out. Now I enrolled him in a much smaller school and its very strict. Very strict! Something he is not use to but its working, less students and more adults involved. There at that school you don't stand a chance. You don't skip, you don't miss, you better not smell like cigarettes or your out. I love it.

Dr. Visit

On April 30, 2012, I had a doctor appointment. I was out of all my medicine so I was glad to be going. When I was in there and the doctor comes in, she explodes, saying I didn't do my labs and that I could have died. She said you could have died overnight on any given day so I will not give you anymore medicine until you do labs. I didn't know that, I certainly didn't want to die. So I left the office and did labs and didn't get medicine for 3 weeks. That was pure torture for me. I thought that was poor judgment knowing I was hurting so bad, but oh well. Again God took care of me and I got over that too. I finally got some medicine on May 16th. It was so tough working with no medicine. Leaving things to God once you did your part is the best thing anyone can do. I'm going to make a change, because I want it and my kids want it. My son James recently hugged me and when he did, he said just stay home. Stay home for about five weeks, and I laughed. I said oh my gosh five weeks!! Talk about me time. I know he meant that with all his heart. He tried making a joke of it. He is the one that wanted me to be a stay at home mom. That I do regret not being able to do. But I'm still not gonna look at it as impossible. Right after my doctor's visit, I called my sister. I was crying. She said, "Just pull over and take control of yourself. Doctors have a way of talking and sometimes they just come across the wrong way. Next time she said she would go with me. And I'm taking her up on that too. I'm just glad I'm so much better now.

THANKS

I grew up in the North Side of Fort Worth. It wasn't always the best neighborhood and it wasn't very easy raising two boys in a rough neighborhood. It took some work, but I did it. Call me crazy, but I love North Side. I'm not ashamed to say that's where I'm from. I think these past few years have worked for me because of my old fashioned rules. I grew up the daughter of a migrant worker. I attended circle park elementary school, J.P. Elder middle school and graduated from North Side High School in 1985. The boys know we will not live in this house forever, but I will tell you one thing, we love the house we live in. It has been a good home for us. No matter if it's in the hood. Plus there's lots of good food around here. Just remember always keep your head up. If you have been feeling down, or had a rough past and don't want to think about it or ever look back, then you have nowhere to go but forward. All three of us thank God everyday for my job. I thank him when I get in my car after every shift. I will never stop thanking him. There is so much to give thanks for. Every morning, every night, my kids, my parents and family, my work family, my customers, and so much more, like cruising. Out of all the great things that God has given me and done for me. If I had to choose one, I would go for the most difficult. *My Job.* It's the one thing that cost me the most tears and pain. I would choose it because as a woman in charge, I chose not to give up. Instead, I thought about who I brought into this world. There were days I wanted to give up. But I just asked God for the strength that I needed every day. Ten years later, I have the strength to lift both my hands to Him and tell Him:

"THANK YOU FOR THE JOB THAT YOU HAD FOR ME."

—Irene Gutierrez